LEADER OF THE PACK

How a single dad of five led his kids,
his business and himself
from disaster to success.

Matt Sweetwood

"America's Single Dad"

Dear Art

Be a leader too!

Best Regards
Matt S.

ISBN: 978-1-54392-473-2

Dedicated to my five successful, kind-hearted, and loving children:

Our journey together has been difficult at times, but our love for one another has brought us through. I wouldn't be half the man I am today without you all. Thank you for raising me.

Matt Sweetwood

CONTENTS

INTRODUCTION

Leader of the Pack is the story of a man who, like many men, had been going through his life apparently content and positively clueless, and who found himself tethered to a tornado as his marriage descended into violence and madness. Surviving courts and cops and chaos, and a crazy-challenging business, he unexpectedly ended up being the only parent of five small children—ranging in ages from only 18 months to 8 years old—at a time when most men didn't even know how to change a diaper.

It is my story.

In it, I detail the transformation I underwent from sole breadwinner and "backup" parent to sole parent, from a beaten abused shell of a man to the strong, confident, and spiritual person I am today, a nationally recognized spokesman for single parents and entrepreneurs.

Though the facts of my story may be different than those of others, my feelings are the same for single fathers everywhere. We are frustrated. We're no longer just the backup parent, the ringer sent in when Mom isn't available—though that was all we had ever been trained for when it came to parenting. It's not that we don't love our children. We do, but that and $5 will get you a latte at Starbucks.

We are told by the many voices of (and silent looks from) counselors, teachers, social workers, judges, and our mothers, sisters, and ex-wives that we aren't as capable of raising kids as a woman. We may even feel that assessment is true. We feel helpless and undermined and, above all, alone in this.

But we are not alone.

A quarter of all American single-parent households are headed by men. We need to own that position, be proud of it, figure out the best way to make it work and, above all, add our voices to a swelling chorus of support for our brothers who find themselves in our shoes.

We must learn to parent like a dad, and that does not mean being only half of a team. In my life, and in the lives of millions of men today, we are the parent. Where there were two, now there is one, and we must be enough.

Lives depend on it…our kids' lives.

We can win our kid's affection and respect, raise them to be happy and healthy people, and manage to have a big, fun, and exciting life while we were doing so. Life isn't over for us. In fact, it is just beginning, and beyond the doors swinging open lies a road we never could have foreseen—one filled with adventure and laughter and even sex.

I surely never would have believed it. On the day my life changed forever, I looked wildly around for any means of escape, but all I saw were their pale and frightened faces, staring up at me. Five little kids. The oldest was only 8, and the youngest still a toddler. My kids—all mine now. Their mother had staged one last violent, terrifying episode and left us forever. Where there were once two parents, there was now only one.

It felt like something had torn a large hole in my chest and ripped out my lungs. I couldn't breathe. Then the breath rushed back in and I heard the most heartbreaking crying. It wasn't until later that I realized the sound was coming from me.

***

Wheaties boxes featured Major League baseball players on them. Barbie dolls had impossibly tiny waists and pointy breasts. Dad might don his checkered apron and silly chef's hat to flip a burger, but holiday dinners were always cooked by Mom. Women had the babies. Men paced the waiting room. The kids' boo-boos got kissed by Mommy, and Daddy got the report of their misdeeds when he came home from work.

That was the world in which I grew up, and though gender lines have blurred (Bruce Jenner is now a woman, for God's sake) and there are enough "Mr. Moms" around for the phrase to be heard less often, not everything has changed, even now.

In the 1980s when my wife and I were having kids, inroads were being made regarding parenting roles. More women were working, and daycare became a normal part of life. But as the man, I was still expected to bring home most of the bacon and as a woman, my wife was expected largely to raise the kids.

We had plenty of those.

My wife stayed home with them, and I went forth to earn the paycheck needed to feed all those hungry mouths. Things unfolded as expected, everybody was relatively happy and healthy...or so it appeared.

Our lives were about to be upended as totally as though an Indonesian tsunami had crashed over us.

My wife, Charlotte, never the nicest woman on the planet, finally dropped the mask she had been hiding behind and revealed her true self to me and to our kids. She was a monster—violent, abusive and downright terrifying. Everything I thought I knew was suddenly a lie, and I found myself struggling to breathe under the weight of her fury, while trying to save my kids without a life vest myself.

I had been her first target in the family. Charlotte belittled me constantly: I was fat and worthless, and I disgusted her. She mocked my manhood and came at me with cutting insults or wheedling endearments, and it was hard to tell which was the most damaging. She hated me, she loved me, she was leaving, I should get out, she couldn't live anymore, I shouldn't be allowed to go on living.

My wife had been increasingly unreasonable, shrieking at the kids over the smallest slights, bellowing like a bully until they were white-faced in a corner, telling them they were useless and stupid and she had never loved them. She hit and kicked walls and the kids, threatening to kill herself. She raged, pivoting between uncontrollable screaming, harsh laughter, and hoarse sobbing. She smashed our lives as surely as she smashed the crockery.

She left in increments—disappearing and reappearing, each time with threats of violence, tormenting the kids, leaving a trail of tears and broken furniture in her wake.

I found myself the single parent of all those children, grabbing for any branch so my children wouldn't disappear in a mudslide of fear and confusion, trying to get up out of the muck myself to be strong for them, trying to work and sleep and provide food and a crying shoulder for my traumatized children and, above all, trying to create order out of chaos.

It was the most important work I would ever do and, hands down, the hardest.

But I strapped one baby to my front, another to my back, grabbed hands, elbows, and shirt collars of the other three kids and started down a road I never thought I'd find myself walking.

Along the way, I found myself in the offices of counselors and clerics, in hot water and nearly in handcuffs, in police stations and political meetings, and in front of many, many judges.

I had no plans to become either a revolutionary or a pioneer—yet I became both. As one of the few who fought the system for years and won, I gave hope to other men fighting for their kids. I had done it. They could do it.

I was asked about my story so often (people gasped at the tale and then passed it around like a box of Cracker Jacks,) I decided to write a little something online about it. I now have many articles that have gotten thousands of views. I had hit a nerve, one as raw and pulsating as mine were when I began this journey. I want to keep sharing my story because it can help people, and I now understand that is why I went through it in the first place.

Leader of the Pack is the story of how our lives fell apart and how I was able to sweep up the pieces and assemble us back into that most unbreakable unit—a strong family. It is the tale of how this single father of five may have lost his hair along the way but not his sanity...or even his sense of humor...and how a newfound spirituality was the greatest treasure unearthed in his journey.

CHAPTER 1
PLAN A

The old saying of, "If you want to hear God laugh, tell Him your plans" just doesn't cut it.

In my case, God was rolling in the aisles...

I had wanted to grow up to be a professional baseball player, earn a great living, meet a beautiful woman who would love me till death do us part, and have a kid who would know, unlike myself growing up, that he or she was wanted and loved, and that I was very proud to be a dad. Not too much to ask, huh?

Apparently, it was.

My life had been the real American Dream, not *The Brady Bunch* kind but the one in which immigrants made it to this new land of promise; changed their name from Zyshlz to Sweetwood to sound less Jewish and blend in better with the WASP establishment; stopped going to temple but kept speaking Yiddish so they could talk in front of their kids without having to spell words; worked their butts off starting a wholesale distribution business; raised two All-American boys, buying them baseball mitts and footballs and paying college tuition; and then sat back to await the joys of being grandparents.

That is the short story version, but it doesn't explain some underlying weirdness that no doubt helped groom me for some relationship wreckage waiting for me in the future.

I was born in 1963, the year *Leave It to Beaver* went off the air, leaving *The Adventures of Ozzie and Harriet* to define the perfect American family. Mine was far from that ideal. True, we had the mom/dad/two kids, but that is where the similarity ended.

To start, we were my father's second family. He had been married before and had other children. (I met them only once, years later in Florida. Dad had been a B-17 bombardier during World War II. After the war, he had returned to his wife and kids, but things hadn't ended well and he had left them. This was long before blended families were the norm.)

He met my mom, the daughter of well-to-do shopkeepers (suppliers of fine whitefish, lox, and cream cheese to the Jewish community in the Flatbush neighborhood of Brooklyn, New York) in 1955. They married, and my brother, David, was born in 1956.

Dad borrowed money from his new in-laws and my mom to start a photographic supply distribution business. He was, in the parlance of any time, a wheeler-dealer. Mom liked that about him. There were whispers in her part of the family that he was shifty and smooth-talking; in Yiddish, a *shyster*—not to be trusted—but Mom fell for his fast-talking ways and thought he was going places. She wanted to go with him. He was the visionary of the pair, the one with wild notions, crazy ideas, and the ability to sell screen doors to submarine owners. Mom was down-to-earth and sensible, and could manage the employees and keep the books. They made a good working team.

All this information—in fact almost all "intelligence" gathered during my whole childhood—came from eavesdropping, snippets overheard, vague impressions, and observation as the precocious kid I was. My father and mother were of a generation (and ethnicity) where personal things weren't discussed, and certainly not with the children. Actually, I never recall my parents' having a conversation about *anything* unless it was about business (which may explain what happened to their marriage later).

Dad had dropped out of City University of New York, where he had studied to be a lawyer (to start making money faster), and Mom, who had been an award-winning student (in the 1930's she was a New York City Spelling Bee champion), believed education was the key to a successful life and drilled that into my skull and that of my older brother.

My brother, David, was tall, handsome, athletic, and a decent student. I wanted to be just like him. I was a short, pudgy, freckle-faced mama's boy with one attribute that got my dad to notice me. When he discovered I could, from a very young age, multiply 123 by 256 in my head, he began to take me with him on his sales calls to show off my skill. It was a bit like being a trained monkey, but I was glad for the attention.

My parents were not absorbed with their kids. Their focus was on their business, and we children were sort of an afterthought. I got the impression, in fact, that my birth hadn't been planned, that I was an accident. That impression was enforced in me when my parents pushed hard to have me bumped up a grade in school, even though the school officials weren't enthusiastic about the idea, realizing I was emotionally younger than my years, not older. Looking back from my adult perspective now, I think my parents wanted me out of the house sooner and my schooling over at the earliest possible date so they could be done with childrearing sooner. They had other things to do and a business to run.

Their business was rolling along smoothly, but their marriage wasn't. My father was having an affair with one of their employees and moved into his own apartment to be with his mistress. Though the mistress eventually left, Dad never moved home. He did, however, come to dinner every night, and the conversations about the business continued as though nothing had ever happened. I knew this wasn't the way my friends' parents ran their marriages, but this odd arrangement was certainly never discussed in my hearing and I surely wasn't about to ask.

The biggest effect of my father's abandonment of his family was that my mom was increasingly sad and turned to me as her only emotional support. She had no friends and didn't encourage her family to gather around her. She grew more isolated and let herself go physically, gaining weight and looking unkempt, as though she wasn't worth any attention, even from herself, after her husband left. She centered her attention on me, but not in a positive way, more as an audience to bear witness to her bitterness and pain.

I tried, in the way of children, to please her. I listened to her complaints, helped her with her household chores, even learned to cook to lift some of her burden, and tried to make her feel less lonely. I felt responsible for her happiness. She cried often and screamed at me a lot, but I never got more than her perfunctory attention. My father got most of what she had to give. She never fell out of love with him.

I was watching the creation of the prototype that would come to mean marriage to me: one partner detached, self-interested, aloof, and independent—even to the point of abandonment; the other needy, obsessed, clingy, and willing to do anything to gain her partner's attention and love. There were no boundaries in my parents' marriage, and there would be none in my own.

But first, I had to survive childhood. I was bullied as a kid, called "Sweet Pea" by my classmates, and avoided getting regular beatings (except one particularly humiliating time when I was attacked with kickballs by the *girls* in my gym class) by giving up every fight before it could start. I fared no better in the classroom, suffering from ADHD before anyone knew it as more than simple inattention. I had trouble reading, but my proclivity for math saved my hide.

My brother, on the other hand, was my parents' favorite, benefitting from the first-born "Messiah syndrome" so well known in Jewish families. (On her deathbed, despite my standing right there by her side, my mother asked, "Where is my son?") David had escaped much of the emotional turmoil of the household by heading off to Rutgers University and then Seton Hall law school to become a lawyer (that occupation my father had quit during his own college years).

I found my own escape in baseball, joining Little League early on and getting to be pretty good at the sport. I was also not a bad football player and was both a low-handicap golfer and a mean pocket pool player—we had a pool table in our basement from the time I was 6 years old. Sports proved to be an equalizer for me. Lots of the kids picking on me were athletes who sometimes wanted me on their team because of my abilities. They had to avoid breaking me into too many pieces in case they needed me to cover a base or catch a pass. The other kids definitely thought me uncool, however. I didn't smoke, drink, or do drugs like many of my classmates, partly because my parents didn't drink or smoke, partly because drugs scared the hell out of me (I believed those filmstrips in health class), and partly because I was younger than all my classmates. They were shaving but I was still collecting baseball cards and playing army in the backyard.

When I wasn't outside, I stayed pretty much in my room. My mother, who once had been a kind and gentle parent, now was the epicenter of many emotional storms, and I closed my bedroom doors against those battering winds. Often, I felt as though I were in a crouch, covering my head, though I learned another protective mechanism when my father was around—I learned to go numb. (This emotional paralysis came in handy then, and I still use it as a shield against some people—mostly women—to prevent them from getting too close to me.) I really felt no love for my father, and tried to erase him from my thoughts when he wasn't there. I do remember when he inserted himself into my consciousness, saying it would be all right if I wanted to become a lawyer like my brother; otherwise, I was expected to join the family business.

I, too, entered Rutgers to study mathematics, and took out a student loan for its low rate of interest. I gave the money to my father to use in the business and he, in turn, paid my college tuition. I lived at home for the first two years, commuting and having no real social life at all. I hung out with other members of the "geek squad," particularly Rob Conner, he of the Coke bottle-bottom glasses and bad skin. We mostly played Dungeons & Dragons or video games and lifted weights together.

I had never dated in high school and could barely talk to girls (despite having a desperate fascination with them and being in "love" a few times). Finally, in my second year of college, I gathered up enough courage to ask a girl out, only to have her announce, in mid-date, she was gay. I didn't try again.

After I got my undergrad degree from Rutgers, I went for my master's degree from the University of Pennsylvania, on a full ride (I didn't want to burden my parents with a big tuition bill), with no firm idea of what I wanted to do with my life (the professional baseball dream had gone the way of all other things when my talent didn't match my desire). I did help with my parents' photographic supply distribution business on weekends, knowing I would eventually inherit it.

Over an intercollegiate math meet at school one fateful day, I met the gaze of a visiting Princeton grad student named Charlotte, and to say she rocked my world is an understatement. She would change the trajectory of my life—making it possible for me to reach the highest heights, while dragging my soul through the lowest pits of hell.

Charlotte had long, curly black hair, piercing green eyes, and a figure like Sophia Loren—she was a true beauty, and I was stunned she would even deign to speak to me. She was smart and Jewish (though why that mattered after my agnostic upbringing, I have no idea), and had grown up in New York in a small town, just like my hometown. I was in love the second she looked my way.

She asked if we could meet for study dates on weekends and I, of course, agreed as fast as I could get the words out of my mouth. We exchanged information about our families and upbringing. Her dad was a traveling salesman, and her mom, a housewife. She seemed intrigued that my folks owned a successful business that I would someday inherit.

Charlotte's own story had some inconsistencies that I thought nothing of at the time.

She had attended Cornell to study physics but had left for an undisclosed reason. She had, perhaps, attended another school besides that one before joining the program at the Princeton. She had a twin brother who had been killed in a car accident but, when I met her parents, I was not to mention that, as the subject caused them too much pain. I thought none of this was odd. I was so euphoric she would even speak with me, she could have told me anything and I would have believed her. So, she did just that—told me anything she pleased, true or not. And I believed her. I dove into our relationship with both feet and no brains.

Soon she seduced me, pretending not to notice my fumbling lack of experience, and shortly thereafter, we were sharing an apartment half-way between our schools. I felt like I had won the lottery. To be living with a woman was the culmination of my wildest dreams, and every morning when I woke up to find her beside me, I felt as though I was dreaming. I threw myself into pleasing her, as I had done with my mom. I handled the household chores, brought take-out for dinner, bought her presents, and helped her with her homework. If she had needed to scrape her boots on something, I would have offered my back. I would happily have literally been her "welcome Matt."

Charlotte took all this attention as her due and, after a while, she began to exhibit spurts of anger at me, which resulted in my redoubling my efforts to make her happy. I never fought back and when she would huff angrily out of the house during an argument, I would chase her down the street, begging forgiveness. The thought of her leaving me was more than I could stand.

When I finally met Charlotte's parents, they loved me. (I learned later they were happy they could foist their lying daughter off on an unsuspecting mark. I had been chosen, not for any lovable characteristics of my own, but because all the other grad students Charlotte could have targeted as her meal ticket through life were poor or Chinese imports.) My parents had nothing to say about Charlotte one way or another. We didn't have personal discussions, and their opinions wouldn't have mattered to me anyway.

Charlotte decided we would be married. (I had not proposed, but I didn't care. If she had decided we would both shave our heads and become Buddhist monks, I wouldn't have objected.) So, when I graduated with my master's in theoretical mathematics, I went immediately to work in my parents' business and used my education to write programs for our very first computer system.. Charlotte quit school, leaving the graduate program early—never finishing the courses required for her to get her Ph.D. (a pattern I learned about later when it was discovered she had been thrown out of previous programs, not left them voluntarily as she had told me).

I had moved back in with my parents and she with hers while we prepared for the wedding. My dad helped me pick out the rings in New York City's Diamond District, and Charlotte went shopping for a couture wedding gown that cost more than my first car.

That wasn't the only thing Charlotte brought to the marriage either.

After telling me that her doctors had told her she would have trouble conceiving (due to some undisclosed and vague "woman troubles"), Charlotte told me that she was pregnant. My heart stopped. I was 23 years old, going on 15, and I panicked at the thought of fatherhood.

"Are we going to keep it?" I squeaked.

"Absolutely. That is not up for discussion," announced Charlotte, and the case was settled.

We told no one what Charlotte called "our delicious secret," and we were married in Tarrytown, New York, on April 18, 1987. What I remember most of that day is that being married meant Charlotte wasn't going to leave me. I cried tears of joy at that thought, not realizing tears would be one of the most permanent results of our union.

***

After a honeymoon at Disney World (the perfect place to embark on a fantasy, I see in hindsight), we settled into a two-bedroom condo in White Plains, right between our respective families. Her parents were delighted at the prospect of grandchildren. My father expressed my family's only opinion, saying he was glad that the honeymoon had been "successful."

To demonstrate the height of normalcy, we even got a dog, a husky-shepherd mix we named Max, who became the apple of Charlotte's eye while we awaited the arrival of our "little bundle of joy."

Charlotte's behavior toward me was changing. She was often cold and brusque, getting very irritated at the slightest thing. I chalked it up to the pregnancy and doubled down on my efforts to please her. She grew chillier toward me and absolutely frigid in the bedroom. She began to pick fights over little things (or nothing at all) and threatened to leave if I spoke in my defense. I learned not to talk back, but soon I was walking on eggshells to avoid upsetting her. It was like living in a minefield. Even Max, the dog, brought her no joy. His care became my responsibility, and he was relegated to an emotional doghouse. I felt like I was joining him there.

On November 3, 1987, our daughter Lauren was born, and Charlotte was ecstatic. She had found her calling, and it was motherhood. From the second our child was born, Charlotte had only one mission and poured every ounce of her manic energy into the baby. On the way home from the hospital, she wouldn't let me speak to or touch the child. She sulked and complained through the entire car ride, and kicked the dog when we entered the condo. "Keep that thing away from us," she yelled.

Adjourning to the nursery, Charlotte wouldn't emerge for hours, speaking to me only when she needed a snack from the kitchen or something to drink. Then she'd issue an order, take the delivery, and slam the door again afterward.

When I tried to talk to her, such an argument would ensue, it's a wonder the paint didn't peel off the walls. Defense on my part was futile. She would hurt me with her words until I was reduced to whispering and whimpering until she stopped.

I always surrendered.

When my mother visited, eager to see her first grandchild, Charlotte would not let her see the baby.

"That woman raised you," Charlotte barked, "and look what a piece of shit you turned out to be."

By this time, I agreed with her assessment of me. I had adopted her belief systems. I *was* a piece of shit, and if I were a better husband, she would be happier. Her contentment was, after all, my responsibility.

Things did de-escalate a little after that. Charlotte became obsessed with being Supermom and was ordering every organic product ever made (no chemical would touch her precious child; she would be vigilant). But all was not peaceful in paradise.

There were early signs something was amiss with Charlotte, but then, "There are none so blind as those who will not see," and I was Helen Keller. She was quick-tempered and demanding. She was too tired to clean. I'd scrub the bathrooms. She had another headache. I'd give her a massage. She needed more money to go shopping, though our closets were filled to overflowing, and out came my credit card. She had to have more shoes, more clothes, and shortly thereafter, more kids.

Yes, I did put kids at the end of the sentence, because it turned out that to Charlotte, our children were just more possessions. They'd eventually get discarded just like last year's handbag. But that was still to come.

The first kid, Lauren, was a delight. Plus, having a baby had the added attraction of making me feel like a manly man. This was for whom I set off into the urban jungle to provide for: my offspring…my woman…my home. I felt like beating my not-too-hairy chest.

Less than six months after the birth of Lauren, Charlotte announced she wanted another baby.

I said no.

Ethan was born on January 26, 1989, 15 months after Lauren's birth. When Charlotte wanted sex, she was a minx and I could not resist her. Sexual enslavement as manipulation got added to the witches' brew of abuse.

I rationalized that getting the childbearing out of the way early meant that we'd still be young enough to enjoy each other when the two kids went off to college and, with Charlotte's problems getting pregnant, maybe it was blessing that we were able to overcome the odds and have two babies so close together.

By the time the third pregnancy was announced, I was beginning to feel the financial pinch and working harder and harder—like a hamster on a wheel—just to keep up. I had no notion of Charlotte's ever going back to work. How could I keep an eye on her if that happened? She was such an amazing catch, I'd surely lose her to another man the second she went out into the working world. But finances were tight and getting tighter. When I timidly proposed we might call it quits after that baby, Charlotte wheeled on me like a Fury.

"I gave up everything for these kids," she raged. "This is what I want to do with my life, and this is what we are doing."

Yes, dear.

Plus, babies are a lot of fun, especially when you aren't the one who is with them all day, and Charlotte saw that I wasn't with them, even on my days off. She was the one raising the children—they were *hers*. I was increasingly relegated to only the roles of ATM and sperm donor. She bought the kids clothes, monitored their activities, chose their friends, determined mealtimes, bath times, and bed times. I barely got to see the kids unless there was a movie on TV she wanted to watch—in which case they were all mine. They were also mine when they had colic, fevers, or nightmares. Mommy needed her sleep, though I was the one up at 7:30 a.m. to go over the company's sales reports and begin my commute to earn our family bread.

When I came home, more often than not, it was up to me to make dinner (or, all too often, to bring home pizza or Chinese). It was also up to me to break up fights around the dinner table—and not all of them were among the kids. Charlotte had favorites and enemies, and who was who changed daily. On some days, our oldest daughter, Lauren, could do nothing right and would rush from the table in tears, only to get invited on the next day to accompany Mom to a private shopping excursion, just the two of them. It was all so uneven, I couldn't keep up, and neither could the kids.

Like all victims of abuse (though I didn't think of myself as one at the time), I would have done almost anything to keep the peace. Living with Charlotte became ever more volatile—like sharing a glass tube with nitroglycerin. An explosion could happen at any minute—and usually did. I was, frankly, scared of Charlotte's moods. I guess you could say I had battle fatigue.

So off we went, Charlotte to play groups and play dates and playgrounds, and me to the high-pressure world of wholesale photographic supply distribution in the wilds of suburban Westchester, New York. I was growing a business, just as Charlotte was so often growing a baby, and the tapestry of our lives unfurled, thread by thread, into what seemed to be the perfect warm blanket of a happy family life.

Then the threads snapped.

The tapestry unraveled with dizzying speed and left us spinning through space untethered.

***

Most of us weren't familiar with terms like "borderline personality disorder" in the 1980s. I might not have heard the words before, but I was living with their expression every day.

After baby number three, Charlotte became more and more hostile to me. She barely spoke to me at all and, when she did take notice of me, it was to pick a fight. I could do nothing to please her. Neither could the babies. When one of them spilled juice, Charlotte would yell at the kid and buy 52 sippy cups to prevent the incident from ever happening again. When one child broke a plate, Charlotte would smash a stack of them on the kitchen floor. Their little butts developed scabs from unchanged dirty diapers (that was another of my jobs when I came home), and when teething pains hit, it was me who walked the floor all night. Charlotte slept on.

The kids knew something was wrong, and they grew pale and eventually silent whenever Mommy walked into a room. Still, somewhere in my mind, I reckoned Charlotte knew more about rearing children than I did. She was a woman and, if you got right down to it, what did I know about anything?

But when Charlotte started talking about baby number four, I put my foot down. No way we were going to have another kid. It would break us.

"Dammit, woman, can't you see what you are doing?" I bellowed.

Okay, so that isn't exactly how the conversation went. It was more like: "Honey, maybe you are carrying too much on your shoulders, and a baby might be too hard for you right now," I squeaked.

Emily was born nine months later.

I got tricked into the fifth child. Charlotte actually agreed to go on the pill and then covertly flushed the contraceptives down the toilet instead of swallowing them. The pill does have a 1 percent failure rate, after all. She claimed we were just victims of circumstance.

Later it was revealed that she had been injecting herself with fertility medications the whole time. (It also was brought to my attention that her uncanny knowledge of newborn care might have been hard-earned knowledge. Lauren might not have been her first child. Charlotte turned out to be four years older than she claimed—something I didn't discover until *after* we separated. And those years of her history were missing—unknown blanks in her adult timeline.)

I was to learn years later, that Charlotte's abusive behavior may have been, in part, caused by her having borderline personality disorder - about which I knew nothing. I was finally told that it means the sufferer lacks identity except through things outside him- or herself. Those things can be an ostentatious mansion, or a Lamborghini or, in Charlotte's case, a brand-new baby to show off.

The title "mother," especially mother to such a brood, won Charlotte validation in the eyes of others and evoked not a little sympathy. "Oh, how do you manage, you poor thing?" people would say (not knowing she had a virtual slave at home to help.)

The problem was that as each baby got older and began to detach from Mommy, that left a hole in Charlotte that could be filled only by the overwhelming love a newborn has for its mother—and so we added to the family each time she felt herself getting hollow.

But when baby number five joined the family, Charlotte, it seems, had finally had enough. Maybe she couldn't take another moment of screaming, unwashed, un-nurtured, un-mothered children, and she started to come apart at the seams.

CHAPTER 2
THE GREATEST SHOW ON EARTH

With that many kids, it was like the circus had come to town and set up its three rings right in our living room. I lived with this menagerie, but I wasn't the glamorous lion tamer, controlling the beasts with a whip and a chair. I was more like the sad little man cleaning up after the elephants.

It's not that I was useless. I could still add endless columns of figures in my head, even without a calculator. I could manage my 100-person company with my eyes closed. I knew how to read a bedtime story and teach a boy to throw a baseball. I was less equipped to create the perfect ponytail, but I could set a Guinness World Record for tying a shoelace. Those lonely years with my mother had even taught me how to roast a chicken, but I was not a domestic wizard, and our house could have used some magic.

I left most of the childcare to my wife. That's what I was taught men do. We were supposed to go out and earn the living. My wife was the one to arrange babysitters—and she would allow only her parents—to watch the kids when we went out. The kids went to Mom when they had a problem or something exciting happened to them at school. The older ones came to me for an occasional game of catch. The baby, Abigail, smiled at me with her two-toothed grin when I walked in, but I don't know that she didn't smile at the mailman the same way. I was a typical father—if with a somewhat abnormally large number of kids.

There were five now—Abigail, Emily, Aaron, Ethan and Lauren—ranging in age from 16 months to 7 years. They were healthy (thank God), rowdy, normal children, if a bit wild and rambunctious.

Our house was noisy, busy, bustling, and, with the addition of each new baby, it devolved into more and more of a pigsty. Charlotte wouldn't clean, nor would she let me hire a housekeeper. It was her kingdom, and I should butt out.

Our home began to look like an episode of Hoarders. Piled laundry, unwashed dishes, garbage everywhere, and, most weirdly, packages of unopened clothes, box after box of shoes, jewelry, towels, toiletries. Charlotte couldn't resist buying them and then wouldn't allow them to be used, so the bags and boxes piled up. In an affluent neighborhood, we were living like hoboes.

This all went against my basic nature, if I still had one buried underneath the rubbish. I am a neat freak, much like Felix Unger in The Odd Couple, and I am uncomfortable in a house that is not clean and tidy. Add noisy and chaotic to the mix, and I feel continually off-balance. I never felt balanced in our home.

The children and I were held hostage by neglect and verbal abuse as Charlotte shrieked and wailed and bellowed and bullied all of us. If anyone talked back, she'd announce she was leaving and we'd stop arguing.

Anything or nothing could set her off on a three-day emotional fit of rage or sobbing. The children did or did not do something. No one gave her any respect. One of us looked at her funny. Any excuse or no excuse was all that was needed for her to throw a tantrum. Every 28 days, I knew to expect a tornado of rage. She went absolutely crazy when she got her period (and was only happy and calm while pregnant).

Her favorite target was me. I was stupid, lazy, and a fat loser, and I disgusted her. She was right about one thing: I was fat. I was an emotional eater, and with the stress about money (we never had enough), worry about the kids, concern about what others would think of us, and the fragile emotional state I was in constantly led me to hide my feelings in food. I ate and ate as though trying to form an armor plate of fat against the constant barrage. I gained one hundred pounds. No wonder Charlotte was disgusted with me. I was disgusted with myself.

Charlotte, on the other hand, had been bulimic since her adolescence and was constantly obsessing over her body. If she didn't like what she saw in the mirror on any given day, we were all in for stormy weather. She always told the girls they were fat and ugly, and I, of course, always I, was sprayed with her venom.

When the warden was unhappy, all the prisoners were in for worse treatment.

We had moved to a huge six-bedroom home in an affluent Westchester suburb, when Charlotte was pregnant with our fifth child, Abigail. This was a house we truly could not afford, but Charlotte insisted, and it never occurred to me to refuse her anything. Combined with Charlotte's unhinged spending, the mortgage and house expenses meant we were in a chronic state of near economic collapse. I had to beg my parents or my brother for more money from the business and had to pile on even more hours at work to even begin to justify the raise.

I was running as fast as I possibly could, but it was as though I was on a hamster wheel. The faster I ran, the more behind I got, and the bills were piling up. I had to take from Peter to pay Paul, and regularly paid part of one bill to stave off creditors on another. Yet still Charlotte shopped, buying entire racks of expensive children's clothes, duplicates of ones she had bought previously, which remained unopened and added to the ever-growing mountain of junk in our house.

No one knew of our situation. To the outside world, we looked all right (or so I thought), and I worked desperately hard to keep it that way. I have since heard that "you are only as sick as your secrets," and I was the self-appointed gatekeeper of the secrets. I told no one what was going on in our home. I felt ashamed, as though it were all somehow my fault that we were living in such a nightmare. I was so in love with my wife and pathetically grateful she would deign to be with me, the bright light of my obsession with her blinded me to the fact that the big top was coming down around our ears.

I was about to be promoted to ringmaster, and I'd be working without a net.

***

I came home one night after a business trip to find all the kids, save one, huddled in the living room. I asked where Aaron was. The kids looked like they had been transformed into pieces of petrified wood. No one answered me. Only the little one's eyes drifted to a hall closet. Following her gaze, I tried the door, but found it locked.

Inside I heard quiet sobbing.

"Aaron, Aaron," I called through the door. "Are you in there?"

Muffled crying was the only sound that greeted me. It was the beginning of Aaron's inability to speak, a reaction to constant trauma that would last for years. When I grabbed a paper clip and jimmied the door open, he fell out onto the floor at my feet. He had not answered his mother's call for him quickly enough, and she had locked him in the dark closet as punishment.

Though Charlotte would smack the kids at the slightest provocation, the real weapon she wielded was the psychological punishment she so frequently inflicted. The kids' wounds were therefore not so visible to the naked eye, but they were just as deep.

Charlotte's behavior was getting stranger, and her fantasies more lurid. She refused to clean the children's clothes. She would buy new ones rather than touch what had touched their skin. She wouldn't bathe the kids, so their hair was lank and greasy and dirt gathered in the folds of their skin. They smelled bad. Their toenails grew so long, they cut the skin of their feet, and the normal scratches of childhood went untreated, so they often had infections. Charlotte didn't make them brush their teeth, and decay set in. Their rooms were a mess, with dirty clothes and unreturned schoolwork mixed together in piles on the floor. Dirty diapers were left where someone had finally taken them off the baby. Dishes and plates were everywhere, as the older kids often foraged for food in the kitchen, sharing with the littler ones. Charlotte told the kids they would have to find their own food—she decided she wasn't feeding them anymore, and emptied the contents of the refrigerator and freezer into the trash.

I would come home at night and try to sort through the mess, feeding the kids something, trying to find clothes that fit for school, and gathering scattered homework, but I was one man standing against a tidal wave of crazy.

Charlotte's mental state grew more precarious. Over the years, she had repeatedly told the kids they were ruining her life. She would leave them the first chance she got, she said, but she had to do so when I wasn't around, as I beat her as punishment for even thinking of leaving. I would beat them too, she told the children, maybe even to death. She might escape me, she said. She might kill herself at any time, and we'd all be sorry when we found her dead. She poured verbal abuse over the kids' heads like hot tar.

"You are stupid and will never be anything but stupid!"

"Why would anyone want to be friends with you, you ugly girl?"

"I never loved you."

"I'm going to kill myself, and it will be your fault."

"You are fat and useless, and I hate even being in the same room as you. You are the worst human being I have ever seen."

That last one was said to me, often.

The problem was, it was true. I was fat and useless—or at least useless when it came to protecting my children. We were on a one-way ride to destruction, but I didn't know how to stop the ride and get off. She was tearing us up, humiliating us, and I was powerless to stop her. I hadn't the backbone...yet.

***

Charlotte began going out at night. When I sheepishly asked where she was headed, I got no answer or a curt, "It's none of your business." She spent hours in front of her makeup mirror before she left, though, and was always dressed to the nines. I began to wonder if she was meeting someone—another man perhaps—and my spirits sank. I made myself sick with worry, envisioning her in someone else's arms. I didn't think I could live through it if she left me.

Mine was a desperate, soul-wrenching love, which may have started out as a healthy emotion but had now become a sick and twisted thing, barren and bleak. I listened for her key in the front door and couldn't sleep until she was safely home. Some nights I didn't sleep at all, as she never came home. I often cried until morning.

Then things escalated. Charlotte began to call me at work and tell me I had to come home early to watch the kids, as she was leaving whether I was home or not. Though my work suffered for it, I always came home.

One day Charlotte announced she was going to return to college and finish her degree. She was going to do this in Manhattan, twenty miles away, and had therefore gotten herself an apartment and was leaving.

The word "leaving" struck me like a bullet in the heart. My worst nightmare was coming true.

I couldn't speak at first and, when I regained my voice, all I could croak out was to beg her to stay. Her answer was no, of course, so I instantly began constructing the fantasy that would allow me to live through her departure. She really was only moving down the road for college, to save time for the commute. She would still be my wife and the children's mother. We would just have to make some adjustments to how we lived. She'd need money, of course, to finance her new apartment, so things would have to get tighter budget-wise. I'd need to hire someone to help with the kids, but surely she would still mother them, and she wasn't leaving forever, and there wasn't another man and...on and on the denial spun until I could breathe again. I wasn't losing Charlotte. I couldn't lose Charlotte. I couldn't live if that were true.

***

It is said God does for us what we can't do for ourselves, and in my case that was certainly true. I couldn't accept that Charlotte was actually gone. I told our children Mommy would be back soon. I had never seen Charlotte's apartment and could therefore pretend it didn't exist. I had never seen the new boyfriend with whom she was living, so he didn't exist either. I held tightly to the fantasy that she'd be back after she got her degree, though I heard nothing more about her schooling, since she had never really returned to college at all.

Actually, I never heard anything at all, because Charlotte didn't speak to me, or any of us, for months. Eventually she did come back a few times, ostensibly to see the kids but in actuality to get more of her clothes, any possessions of any worth from the house, and even food from the refrigerator to take back to her apartment.

On one of these occasions, I got a call from Charlotte at my workplace. She was staying with the kids for the afternoon, as I had begged her to do in my pathetic, misguided attempt to get her to come home to live—to come home to love me.

"Oh, Matt," she choked out through sobs, "I've done something awful."
"What, what did you do?" I asked.

"I've hurt Ethan," she said, and the call was disconnected.

Ethan was our 7-year-old.

I couldn't get home fast enough. With a pounding heart, I drove through every red light in Westchester. I ran into the kitchen and found Charlotte, crying hysterically, with her head down on the kitchen counter. Ethan was in the corner with blood streaming down his face. His older sister Lauren was using a towel to stanch the bleeding. I pieced together the story from the other kids who had seen it happen.

Charlotte had been screeching at Ethan over some minor infraction. Knowing from experience that anything he said would only add fuel to her fire, Ethan tried to get out of the room as quickly as possible. He was too late. A coffee mug had sailed through the air and shattered on his head.

When I turned to Charlotte for some explanation, her crying stopped as though a faucet had been turned off.

"It slipped from my hand," she said with an oddly vacant smile.

It was as though time went into slow motion. I looked at my kids, trembling in the corner of the room—I could actually see them visibly shaking—and saw the stark fear in their eyes—fear of this monster who looked like their mother. I watched the blood run down my son's face, and I had a moment of clarity. Something clicked in me, like a key in a rusty lock. I felt my spine stiffen. The truth hit, and denial fell off me like shards of broken glass.

I told Charlotte to go back to her apartment and that I would clean up the mess.
"You are a piece of sh——," she replied, and walked out the door.

When Charlotte walked out, my knees gave way, and I sat down—hard. I felt cold, then hot, then started shaking uncontrollably. I was going into shock.

"Get a hold of yourself," a quiet voice within me said, "You've got to go comfort the kids."

I got unsteadily to my feet and managed to take in enough air to talk to the kids. I took the towel from Lauren's hands and washed and bandaged Ethan's head.

I reluctantly asked Lauren and Ethan the question I already feared I knew the answer to.

"Has your mother physically hurt you before?"
Lauren shook her head affirmatively. Ethan responded, "Of course she has many times. How could you not know? She twists our arms almost to the breaking point, she kicks us with her favorite L.L. Bean hiking boots, and we wouldn't have done anything to deserve that. Check Aaron's leg right now. He has a bruise on it from her kicking him the time she got mad when he didn't pick up the phone fast enough."

I finally saw clearly.

Things weren't going to get better. Things were never going to get better with Charlotte.

But they could—and must—get better for my kids.

I considered, and swiftly rejected, the idea of calling the police. I knew the cops would show up and ask what happened, and Charlotte would calmly lie through her teeth.

"My husband beat me, he kicks our kids and bloodied our son," she'd wail, her eyes flowing with buckets of convincing tears.

My kids, the only witnesses to the truth, would be asked what really happened and risk literally getting themselves killed for speaking out against their vengeful mother, or have to agree with her lies, in which case I would go to a cell. My kids would be unprotected in an increasingly dangerous situation. So, like some rape victims and other people who have suffered violence at the hands of others, I shut up...but I didn't shut down.

Charlotte didn't return home then, but she did return occasionally, not to reunite with us, but to wreak more havoc. But something in me had come alive that day...the will to fight...the balls to stand up to this horror. My kids needed me, and I would be there for them, no matter what it took.

What it would take would be more than all my time and all my money. This fight would consume all of my soul.

From that day forward, I was going to be a single father to my kids, and we were all going to make it...together.

CHAPTER 3
RAISING A PARENT

None of us makes it much past the age of 11 before we get squeezed like putty through a Play-Doh factory into what society deems the proper shape of a boy and a girl. Pretty soon, those shapes harden to concrete and we find ourselves fully formed men and women.

I was pretty sure I was set. I knew what was expected of me, what I had to do to be a man—even a good one. I was kind (most of the time), charitable (as long as it involved only money, not an emotional investment), thrifty (I could squeeze the buffalo off a nickel.), trustworthy (I didn't cheat on my wife. Even if it had occurred to me, I wouldn't have dared.), and loyal (I always was available to listen to the woes of my friends.). That was me—a veritable Boy Scout in many ways, but the one motto I had not adopted from that esteemed organization was, "Be Prepared."

Naturally, I couldn't have seen what was coming, but what was I thinking by knowing virtually nothing about cooking, sewing, cleaning, first aid, my kids' teachers and friends, what Emily was frightened of, or what Aaron was worried he'd never be good at? How could I have been so totally unprepared to meet any of my children's emotional needs or help them face their fears or glory in their accomplishments? Because I thought it wasn't my job, that's why. That was her job. But she had told us to take that job and shove it. She wasn't working here no more.

I would have to learn not only to be a breadwinner but to be a parent—with all the chest-cracking openness of heart that required.
***
My problem was partially one of my preconceptions. My father was my first role model of what a father should be and, to put it mildly, he was no nurturing diaper-changer. If the truth were to be told, neither was my mother devoted to being an earth mother or a domestic goddess. Both of my parents were too focused on work, and they shared one other singular interest: both of them were focused on my father. I remember how my brother and I spent part of our time with my mother. We would sit by the front window of our house and watch the passing cars. We'd guess how many cars would go by before my father would park his Fleetwood Cadillac (he always bought the biggest car on the market) and come home for dinner. It was my mother's favorite game, because she was so excited to see him and could barely wait for his arrival every evening. (I pretended to be

26

excited and felt guilty about the pretense, as I really didn't want him to come home at all. He scared me.)

For my father's part, if he felt any familial duty at all, it was to earn money and be successful at business. He wasn't a help to my mother in her parenting or household duties—that was her job, and eventually mine (self-adopted) as a boy.

So, I grew up, as most men of my generation, believing women did the rearing and raising of children. (This was reinforced by my wife, who barely let me near my own kids.) Somewhere in the 1980s, this world started to change. We, as a culture, thought it was still unusual enough to have fathers care for their kids in 1983 that Michael Keaton made a pile of money on a movie entitled Mr. Mom, detailing the hysterical premise that a man could actually stay home and care for his kids while his wife went to work. But I was already a young man by then, and my duties and responsibilities in any future marriage were pretty set in my mind. When it came to my own marriage, I made the money (and more of it was required all the time), and my wife raised the kids.

The system was breaking down in our household in those last days, of course. No one was keeping the house or raising the kids, and my bumbling attempts to salvage the situation during weekends and my odd moment home from my accelerating duties at work were only Band-Aids on a hemorrhage.

My own mom offered whatever help she could in her moments away from work, but my wife wasn't having any of that. My brother had his own family to worry about, and we had to keep this burgeoning disaster a secret from the neighbors, so my sense of isolation grew.

I recently read a piece of Jewish wisdom that states, "Seek out one true friend in your life. Make it a goal to find someone you share everything with," and I thought back over the years. My dad had such a friend, Doctor Harry Melman. He was my father's best friend his entire life and, though I was never privy to what went on between them, I know my father relied on that friendship. Doctor Melman always had his back—no matter what happened with my father's wife, his mistress, or his children. Such a sounding board would have proven invaluable to me, I think, though I never broke my childhood cycle of loneliness and having few friends. In this I emulated my mother.

My wife, at least in my eyes, was my best friend—in fact, my only friend. Though with the perfect clarity of vision that is hindsight I know she was in fact no friend of mine in any way, at the time her pulling away from me felt like one of my limbs was being ripped off. Without her, I had no friends. Without her, I was adrift.

I am still a man with few friends, but I do have five close ones: my children. But in those tumultuous early years, the kids were just flying objects on the periphery of the tornado of my life. I wasn't trying to relate to my children on any level except that of animal handler. I was trying to get them in line and quiet the noise.

I couldn't cut through the screaming (Lauren), dramatic sobbing (Emily), outright defiance (Ethan), or human whirling dervish that was Aaron. Baby Abigail carried her own mess with her like the cloud that follows Pig-Pen in the Peanuts comic strip. I was reduced to just trying to keep my head above water in this sea of shorter humans, and I was constantly under threat of drowning. I once no sooner had Abigail out of her diaper than I heard a crash upstairs. Aaron had run by a bedside table, tripped over the cord, and smashed a lamp to pieces. Ethan smacked him in the head and, as he had pulled back his hand to do so, had accidently hit Emily, and the crying began anew. Her tears ducts were always overflowing. Lauren, ever the most dramatic, would fling herself on the bed (thus throwing everything piled on it onto the floor to do so) and scream over some unspoken daytime drama in her head. All of this would escalate, and still no one was dressed for school and I was already late for work.

There were a couple of unspoken contracts at play here, I realize now. I had decided, long ago when I was myself a child, that when I got married and had children, I would be extra loving and kind to them. Unlike me with my father, my kids would never be afraid of me, and their only fear would be of disappointing me. This last clause was based on their huge respect for me, respect I would earn, of course, by being the kind, loving father heretofore mentioned in clause one of this fantasy contract.

The second unspoken contract was the one with my wife: we would have the kids, and the division of labor would be such that I would make the money and she'd raise the children. This contract would continue until the last child was 18 years old, and then my beautiful wife would morph into my perfect companion—not a love slave (though continued nonprocreating sex would be nice) nor as someone catering to my every whim, but as a loving partner. We would care for each other, maybe travel together, enjoying the fruits of our labors into a serene and financially secure old age.

Leader of the Pack

The problem with these contracts was that no other parties had actually signed on to them. The kids were unaware of my affectionate patriarch role and their place within that identity I was creating for myself in my mind. My wife had broken the contract about her even taking care of the kids; forget the part about us and that serene old age we'd share. Charlotte was on strike, and I was the scab crossing her picket line to keep the factory running. I wasn't even given a verbal two weeks' notice when she quit her job, and I went on believing, even after she moved out, that she would, at least in some capacity, hold up her end of the contract. I didn't realize that if a contract had ever existed except in my imagination, she had torn it up and flushed it, and us, down the toilet.

***

I didn't have time to sit down, take a breath, and think the matter through. Everything I did was a reaction as opposed to a response to the chaos around me. My attention was always getting diverted by the next crash, yowl, or scream, and no task got my full attention. Even my business was suffering from my distraction. It was like trying to keep a dozen plates spinning and watching them smash, one by one, on the ground around me.

I took to clotheslining Aaron as he ran by or grabbing him by the back of the collar and holding him aloft as he struggled, while I held a wriggling Baby Abigail on my hip. I often corralled the baby before she could insert that paper clip into her mouth or the electrical outlet. I tried recruiting the girls to pick things up, as I rarely had a free hand, but screaming orders at them resulted only in a flood of tears. Neither girl moved except to fling herself to the floor in a storm of weeping. Ethan's only reaction to things seemed to be to punch them. Before Charlotte left, I'd sheepishly ask her if she could put the dishes (stacked to overflowing in the sink) in the dishwasher. She'd answer me either by breaking them or throwing them away and buying more.

I often felt like I was going insane.

When I heard myself threaten the life of Aaron for being late for school due to him losing his shoes for the seventh time that week, I knew something had to give. I just didn't know what to do or where to begin to make any changes. I had the fleeting thought it would be better if I just burned down the house and started all over again. I also had the more-than-fleeting thought that I should run away and join a foreign baseball team or relocate to Paraguay and leave no forwarding address. I, of course, did none of those things but like a kettle set to boil, I did start to overflow with feelings, and they began spurting out.

Before Charlotte left, I cried at night, particularly when she was out and I didn't know where. Those, I now realize, were tears of self-pity—understandable, but not very helpful. The other tears, the ones that poured out of me when she finally left, those were tears of fear. I was terrified most of the time. What would I do without her? What would the kids do without their mother? How could I care for them? What would become of us? What did the future hold? Without her, did I even have a future? Did I want one?

I now know that such tears are not only forgivable but mandatory. Without such a release, I might have legitimately cracked up, and then where would my kids be? Also, I know that there is no getting around fear or stuffing it down. It just roars back up and can consume your life. I needed to feel it, and all those negative emotions, until I could face the fear, walk through it, and ever so slowly realize I had made it through to the other side. But that was in the future. At that time, the tears helped wash away only the tiniest bit of the pain, giving me just a breath of relief, so I could keep going. Still, every morning, after many sleepless nights, my feet hit the floor like they were made of lead. I gritted my teeth, set my jaw, and literally dragged myself through another day.

I never let my kids see me cry. That was part of the manhood mask I grew up with. Men didn't show their emotions; we soldiered on and channeled whatever we felt into screaming for our sports teams and working ever harder at our businesses. But bottling up all my fear and sadness and trepidation about the future didn't work. I needed a vent for that steam to escape, and I found myself actually sharing the big secret of our disintegrating home with someone who had only recently come into my life.

I found myself complaining about my situation to one of the new employees I had hired away from a competitor of ours on the West Coast.

Idan was an Israeli salesman, possessed of an empathetic nature and a sympathetic ear. He would turn out to be a good friend, and he would teach me a lesson I didn't even know I had to learn: it is okay to ask for help. We as humans, even male ones, aren't equipped to handle everything all by ourselves. He would offer a helping hand—one that would become an absolute lifeline to me.

After listening to my increasingly desperate descriptions of what was going on at our house, he asked some questions, and I answered like a perfectly programmed automaton.

Why didn't I have a housekeeper? he asked. Oh no, my wife won't allow anyone else to help her run the home. How about a nanny or an au pair to help with the children? Charlotte will allow only her parents to babysit the children, I parroted. He kept asking, and I kept spouting the (irrational) party line as fed to me by my wife until even I began to hear how ridiculous my answers sounded. Charlotte wasn't running the home. No one but me was helping with the children, and I wasn't doing much helping. And my wife had one foot out the door.

I finally wound down my ludicrous explanations and only then (smart man) did Idan propose a solution. He knew someone who brought Israeli women into the country as nannies. And that connection would provide me with young Israeli women who would jump at the chance to come to America and act as nannies to my unruly brood. He even pointed out that all young people—male and female in Israel—were required to spend time in the army, and he referred to two potential candidates who were battle-hardened veterans not likely to be frightened off by my erratic, hostile wife. They would, he assured me, stand their ground.

They could help with cooking, cleaning, and laundry as well as childcare, Idan said, and they wouldn't cost that much—just room and board in my very large house, plus a stipend. If I liked, he would contact them right away. Upon hearing that news, I felt like I was able to take the first deep breath I had taken in months.

I felt that breath choked off a second later when I realized what Charlotte would say, on one of her trips back to the house, when I told her the news. The explosion, I was sure, would be heard around the world. But desperate times call for desperate measures, and I was truly desperate. I'd have to brave the storm to save our ship from sinking. I swallowed hard and told Idan to make the call.

CHAPTER 4
THE CAVALRY ARRIVES

I had confessed to my new friend, Idan, that given the state of insanity in my house, I had contemplated calling 1-800-Nanny but didn't know how to explain that whomever I hired should come with a shovel, a dumpster, a gas mask, and full-body armor, as there was a very real possibility she might need to defend herself against my wife.

In 1948, the interim government of Israel called for the establishment of one unified military that was called the Israeli Defense Forces (Tzhal). Its job was to fend off invading Arab enemies.

From the age of 18, every male and female Israeli is required to serve three or two years, respectively, of compulsory military service. Young women are fully trained for combat. Courses in weaponry, survival, and battle strategy ensure that the IDF turns out some tough cookies, not likely to back down in the face of a formidable enemy. I was very glad to hear that, as I knew Charlotte to be formidable and, anticipating her response to the hiring of the nannies, I was fairly certain she would consider them enemies.

I wasn't disappointed in that expectation.

"You did what?" Charlotte bellowed when I told her I had engaged the services of not one but two young women to help me handle the house and children. "You are letting strangers come in my home and touch my children! You sneaky, conniving piece of sh—! If you think I am going to let this happen, you are dead wrong! I'll...I'll..." and the rest was lost to incoherent mutterings, punctuated by many world-class obscenities—a tirade I was becoming used to, as almost anything could send her off on one.

In the end, the nannies came anyway. Charlotte, by this time, was gone back to her apartment, which was a physical relief, even if I was still being held prisoner by her emotionally. At least the new dishes I had to buy after her last rampage might stay un-smashed now. The fact that my spirit felt broken was shown in the apparently permanent slump of my shoulders, but I carried on. I didn't know what else to do.

Then came the day I was to pick up the new nannies. Shira was first. I got a message that I was to pick her up at the Harlem YMCA on 135th Street in Manhattan. She had arrived from Israel the day before and was directed to the Y because it had some of the cheapest rooms available in the city. For a girl who had never left Israel before, it must have been a terrifying experience to fly into bustling JFK, find and board a bus into Manhattan, and make her way to what was then not the best neighborhood in the city.

She later told me she had spent the night locked in her sparse room, quaking in terror and not sleeping a wink. When I showed up to get her, she—whom I later discovered was normally shy and quiet—could barely utter a peep.

For my part, I saw a petite and pretty young woman in her early 20s, with long, dark hair, olive skin, and enormous eyes. Her slender frame gave no hint of her inner toughness and, looking at her, I was hoping she was small but sinewy, and very well trained by the military to never back down in the face of enemy fire. Otherwise, I foresaw her getting mowed down by Charlotte, on one of her trips back into the house, and catching the next plane home to Tel Aviv.

I gathered her one bag and led her to the car. During the drive to Westchester, I tried to engage her in conversation, but she was crying softly and visibly shivering. She had no winter coat, so I cranked up the heat and lent her mine. Then I tried to converse with her again. I could get out of her only that she had come from a large family and knew a lot about babies. That, I thought to myself, would have to do.

When we pulled up to my house, Shira's eyes got even bigger. She looked at the huge house and gulped audibly. She later confided she had never seen a place half so big. It reminded her of a palace. Hailing from tiny Israel, she couldn't believe one family got all that space to themselves. But she straightened her shoulders and marched bravely out of the car.

Charlotte, thank God, was not, as I half feared, lying in wait at home when we arrived, and Shira got to meet all the kids without being intimidated by my wife. Ethan was curt, ducking his head to say a quick hi before running off. Aaron said nothing—as was no surprise to any of us in the family; he seriously had barely spoken a word in nearly a year. He just stared at Shira from under his fringe of hair and ran to his room. The girls both looked Shira over (like women have done to other women from time immemorial) and then Emily shyly said, "hi."

But it was Baby Abigail, riding in Emily's arms, who had the most surprising reaction. She took one look at the new nanny, gave a wide, toothy smile, and stuck both her chubby arms out to Shira, who smiled right back and instinctively grabbed Abigail for a hug.

Theirs was a love at first sight and one that would prove to be unshakable.

If the kids had been older, this thawing of relations might have taken longer (I shudder to think what would have happened had they all been adolescents), but as they were young, they couldn't resist the urge to show off and couldn't hide their curiosity about this new stranger in their midst.

The kids followed Shira to her room and, once she had dropped her bag, proceeded to give her a tour of the house—their rooms in particular, followed by the TV room and the kitchen (the places dearest to their hearts). I watched as she went, seeing her eyes take in the mountains of trash and laundry, the broken toys everywhere, and the sink piled high, as always, with dirty dishes. I started to apologize for the mess, but even though she was a quiet little thing herself, the wave of her hand was regal and spoke volumes. "It doesn't matter, Mr. Matt," she nearly whispered. "It will all be made right."

I didn't believe her, but I desperately hoped she was correct.

The next day, I set off to the Port Authority Bus Terminal in Manhattan to pick up the other nanny, Yael. She, too, was only 21, but the second I saw her stride out of the station, with her muscular frame, strong jaw, and direct glance, I knew she was the physically tougher of the two young women.

She stuck her hand out first, shook mine firmly, and told me she was glad to meet me. She also said she was eager to meet the children, and asked right off, "Shall we go?" We did and, unlike Shira, Yael asked a million questions on the way home—about the kids, their schedule, and even their mother. I tried to answer as directly as the questions were asked but stammered over some of the explanations. How could I explain Charlotte's actions to Yael when I couldn't even explain them to myself?

When we pulled up to the house, Shira and the kids were waiting for us. Yael and Shira exchanged greetings, involving one of the few Hebrew words I knew, "shalom" meaning "peace." I hoped it would prove to be the state of things. Yael greeted each of the kids by laying a light hand on their heads as though in blessing, but when she and Emily locked eyes, it was as though they had known each other forever. Theirs was a special bond that never failed, and I saw it form with that first glance.

Once shown into the house and having put her things away in her room, Yael was given the same tour as Shira, but her reaction wasn't as subdued. Yael walked the house with loud tsk-tsks, audible sighs, and head shakes.

"This will never do," she said. "There is much work to do."

I said, "I'm sure you are tired from your long flight. Tomorrow we can go shopping for whatever you need."

She nodded curtly at me but said to Shira, "Let's get started now."

The two women herded the kids upstairs, leaving me standing in the hall, and I wondered what I should be doing. My question was answered when Shira came down the stairs and said to me, "Yael said to take you into the kitchen and make you a cup of tea. She will be down in a few minutes, after she gets the kids started on cleaning their rooms, to talk over what happens next."

That sit-down at the kitchen table was one of hundreds we would have over the next couple of years.

Yael, obviously a master organizer, had determined that Shira would handle most of Baby Abigail's care, while Yael herself would deal with the older kids. A rapid-fire conversation in Hebrew between the two women came next, with them agreeing to the scheduling of the next steps.

"First, Mr. Matt, we have to deal with cleanliness," announced Yael. "We are now going to cut the children's hair and then wash each one in turn. The children are very dirty, and we will need cloths and towels—many of them. We also will need a nail clipper. Tomorrow we will go buy small scissors and a manicure set—but the boys' toenails are digging into their skin right now and must be cut."

I nodded and ran to open some unopened towels and washcloths, another of Charlotte's crazy over purchases. Then I went into my bathroom and loaned them my nail clipper. I found scissors in the kitchen drawer for the hair trims, and Yael produced a brush and comb.

"We will bathe or shower each child while we are washing sheets for each of their beds, and we will also launder pajamas and clothes for their school tomorrow," said Yael.

I told her we had plenty of sheets and pajamas not yet opened, freeing her and Shira to use two of the house bathrooms to wash the kids. I dug up toothbrushes and toothpaste out of the various bathrooms (Yael shook her head at the state of the toothbrushes, and new ones went on the shopping list she'd begun), and the battle of tooth-brushing began after the bathing was over. It was a pitched battle. The kids were not used to taking orders—especially over dental hygiene—but Yael was unmoved and, like with all such fights that would happen in the future, she wore her opponents down until she had won the day.

Scrubbed, bathed, and smelling much better, with fresh beds and in clean PJs, the kids were brought down to the table for cups of hot chocolate (made with milk) and some quick biscuits Shira had thrown together from leftover Bisquick, the remaining egg in the house, and a dribble of milk.

"The children are hungry, Mr. Matt," explained Yael, "and they will sleep better if their stomachs are full."

When she asked, "Does anyone want to hear a story before bedtime?" I thought for sure there would be an open rebellion about "We wanna watch TV" or "We aren't going to bed, and you can't make us." To my surprise, they trailed Yael up the stairs like ducklings. Structure, I would learn, makes children feel safe.

Shira took the newly clean and diapered Abigail up to rock with a bottle while she sang, and nighttime, usually a time of terror, descended on the house, wrapping us in what seemed suspiciously like a warm blanket.

I slept better that night than I had in months.

The first month or so was spent with my helping them figure out my work schedule, the kids' team and club times and locations, arranging drop-offs and pickups at school, teaching them to use the credit cards I got them, acclimating them to the grocery store (which was a bit like when Robin Williams faced hundreds of kinds of coffee in Moscow on the Hudson), and even explaining American TV and its hundreds of channels.

Once they got their sea legs, a schedule had to be established, and we set one up that could have passed muster in a military organization. I did a lot of the baseball/soccer/after-school-activity transport, and Shira and Yael handled most of the on-the-scene domestic duties. We became a great team, and things began to settle down in the house.

***

It took a solid month of work to get the house itself physically in order. Yael and Shira devised a schedule encompassing every task that needed to be done and a list of supplies they would need: garbage bags by the score, disinfectants, deodorizers, cleaning and laundry products, brooms, mops, and a new vacuum (our built-in wall vacuum system, though apparently never used, had bitten the dust. I was pretty sure Ethan and Aaron had tested it by vacuuming up small woodland creatures). Tubs and showers needed to be scoured, old food scraped out of the refrigerator, and the freezer defrosted with the help of a rubber mallet. The garage needed to be cleared to make room for the little purple Toyota RAV4 I got the nannies so they could run errands while I was at work. Broken toys needed to be thrown out, and old books given to the library. The piles of unopened new clothes were sorted and returned to the Gap, Lands' End or L.L.Bean for partial credit. There were so many of these items, the stores held special half-price sales of them. Used clothing was cleaned and made ready to give to the poor, and it was Yael who asked if we could give the things away to a young family she knew from a Brooklyn synagogue. "Sure," I said, not knowing that choice would prove important in my life later on.

My own clothes were finally cleaned and pressed, and everyone went to get professional haircuts. The kids also got taken to the pediatrician and the dentist for checkups, and were put on a regular maintenance schedule.

The pantry was restocked. (Charlotte had gone on food "kicks"—either everything had to be organics and fresh kale only, or she'd mix some tap water into a Kraft mac-and-cheese boxed meal and call it dinner. It was, like everything else in her life, all or nothing at all.) Now hot, nutritious meals were prepared, and we all sat down at the table as a family to eat. The nannies required napkins and silverware to be used (no more eating with one's hands) and, under Yael's strict eye, manners began to make an appearance. The first time Ethan said, "Can I have some more potatoes, please?" I almost fell off my chair.

All the kids, on their clean sheets and finally with a sense of security, began to sleep long and deeply. Even the baby managed to make it through the whole night when her teeth weren't bothering her. When they were, frozen teething rings, prepared just for that eventuality, were pulled from the freezer by Shira.

Things weren't perfect, however. There was, always lurking on the edges, the fly in our particular ointment—Charlotte.

She had moved out in October of 1996, but returned several times to terrorize us all. She made quite an impression the first time she met the nannies.

"Where the hell are they?" Charlotte's voice blasted me out of bed before dawn. "I want to see them right now!"

Her screeching voice woke the kids too. The baby started screaming. Emily began her daily crying. The boys scrambled down the stairs, trying to avoid getting smacked for some unspecified offense, with Ethan mocking his mother under his breath. Lauren ran to see what craziness her mother was up to.

"Get away from me," Charlotte snarled. "I don't want to see you. I want to see those bitches your father hired to get rid of me."

Yael came out into the kitchen, wrapping a robe around her, trailed by a sleepy-looking Shira. Yael didn't look sleepy at all. She looked, with her black hair untied and streaming behind her, as though she was girded for battle.

"Mrs. Sweetwood, I am Yael and this is Shira. We are here to help care for your house and your children. It is a pleasure to meet you," she said, sticking out her hand.

"Pleasure, my ass," Charlotte screamed, slapping Yael's hands away. "I want you out of my house right now!"

Yael turned and took Shira by the shoulders, turning her too, then looked back at the kids and said, "Come on, children, let's get dressed for the day," and the two nannies led the kids out of the room. Charlotte barely seemed to notice. She wheeled on me, threw a juice glass at my head, and shrieked, "I want them out. I want them out now. Either they go or I go…"

I took a deep breath and said, "Honey, we need some help around the house and with the children just until you are done with school…"

"You are trying to replace me," Charlotte screamed, purple in the face now. "Well, if you think you can replace me, you're about to learn a thing or two," and she smashed another glass as she ran out the door. I heard the tires squeal, and turned wearily to sweep up the glass yet again. Shira reached around and took the broom from my hand. "I'll take care of that, Mr. Matt. You go get ready for work." And I did.

***

I would get calls from Yael during my workday. "Mr. Matt, your lovely wife is here," she would say. She always referred to Charlotte as "your lovely wife," her voice dripping with sarcasm.

"Your lovely wife is here, demanding we leave and throwing things around the living room," Yael would report. "Since the children are here, Shira and I are going to take them somewhere until after you get home."

And off they'd go…to the grocery store, or a park, or the mall, and I would drive home to take the brunt of Charlotte's latest paranoid fantasies and violent threats.

"You are sleeping with those women you brought into my house, aren't you, you sick pervert?" she'd wail. "Your whores are trying to turn my babies against me, and it's not going to work because I am onto your games."

"Charlotte, honey, it's not like that," I'd explain, not understanding I was arguing with a disease. "They are only here to help until you have more time and can come home. Nobody could take your place. You are their mother and my wife, and I don't want anybody else."

That was still true, despite her behavior and what I suspected she was doing with other men. I did love only her and wanted only her love in return. I wanted whatever was the matter to just go away, and have her come back to me and our kids. I was bloodying my fists beating against a stone wall that would not budge and through which I couldn't see a crack of light.

The fights, and her threats, began escalating: "I'm going to kill you," she'd rage or, "I'm going to kill myself and it will be your fault."

She never made good on either of those threats, obviously, but I still hoped she would calm down or that I could help her fix whatever was wrong and she could come home.

I was, of course, hoping in vain.

CHAPTER 5
COPS AND CUFFS AND PUTTING ON THE CAPE

The whole thing made me wonder: Was Batman ever tempted to ignore the Bat-Signal? Did Clark Kent ever consider just putting his head down on his Daily Planet typewriter when the call went out for Superman?

Most days, I felt like crawling under a rock and sleeping for a million years. The whole prospect of my future seemed like a life sentence: 18 years or more during which my entire existence would be tied to this pack of children, and I would be alone, unequipped, inept. The road stretched out in front of me like an endless dirt track through a desert.

What if Charlotte didn't come home?

The thought so paralyzed me, I had to learn to push it aside. That took an almost physical act of will, but I couldn't move while that thought obsessed me, and I had to keep moving. My kids were still growing. My life was moving along. Like it or not, I had to go with it, even though I felt more like a log being dragged upstream than a kayaker steering through the current.

I was about to get some aid though, in a less visible way than I might have liked, but a spiritual helping hand nonetheless.

Shira came to me one day and asked why I had no mezuzah on the house's door lintel. A mezuzah is a small ornamental piece of wood or metal that contains a tiny scroll calling for a blessing upon an observant Jewish home and its occupants. I had no answer except that I hadn't been raised with any particular devotion to Jewish practices.

Shira said firmly, "Well you need one, and I don't want to be in a house without one." I went right out to the local Judaica store, looked curiously at all the other Jewish items I had little clue about, bought a mezuzah, and came home and installed it. Shira helped me say the prayer. Those were the first words of Hebrew I had ever spoken. I never touched my fingers to the mezuzah as one is supposed to do upon entering the house, but I never failed to look at it every time I came home.

It somehow gave me comfort.

Yael and Shira's presence helped me in other ways too. I didn't feel as though I was the only adult in the house anymore (admittedly, some days, I didn't feel like an adult at all). Oddly, though Charlotte was a constant thorn in the nannies' sides, both of them were calm, collected, and even compassionate about her. She kept coming in and out of the house to get her things as she moved out in fits and starts. Sometimes she took her things. At other times, she weirdly took some of the kids' things. She occasionally slashed my things. She mostly wreaked havoc with her visits.

Yael confided in me that she knew Charlotte was a sick woman and therefore, while it was important to keep the kids away from her as much as possible, it was not necessary to be angry at her for her behavior. The nannies treated Charlotte as though she were a landmine in the Sinai— something to be aware of and avoided.

One of those mines was about to explode.

It all started with a stolen car.

Parked safely in my garage was a 1996 BMW E36 M3 coupe—a two-door glowing silver sports car, the last remnant of my campaign of spending more than I could afford in order to give my wife the lifestyle she fervently believed she deserved. Though it helped push me down the rabbit hole toward bankruptcy, I loved that car. (I read the other day that a man enlarged his home's front door so he could park his BMW in his living room during a hurricane. I, and every other BMW owner, understand that man's motivations perfectly.)

I was at work one day, trying to earn enough to feed my kids and pay for Charlotte's compulsive spending sprees, two nannies, and the big lifestyle we were living as well as an extra car payment (I had bought the nannies a Toyota RAV4, as mentioned, in addition to the eight-seat Chevy Suburban we already had, so they could divide up the kids and take them to after-school activities, the grocery, the library, and wherever the nannies' chores took them), when I got a call from Yael.

Charlotte had returned to gather up more of "her stuff," slamming into the house, shrieking wildly, and being apparently very angry about some situation, real or imagined. The kids hadn't returned yet from school and, knowing how violent Charlotte could become, I told Yael to take Shira and get out of the house. Then I left work and went home to see what was going on with Charlotte this time. I was hoping she would just scream at me for a few minutes and then leave so the kids could return to a peaceful home.

As I pulled into the driveway, I saw the garage door slowly open, and Charlotte walked out with the extra set of BMW keys she had taken from the key hook in the foyer. She knocked on the window of my car (I was driving the Toyota RAV4 that day) and, with an ugly sneer, shook the keys at me. "You love this car, don't you? You love this car more than you love me. I think you need to be taught a lesson. When I am dead and this car is gone, you'll be sorry then," she snarled.

As her words were sinking in, she turned, ran, and jumped into the driver's seat of the BMW. Turning on the ignition, she blasted out of the garage at a rate of speed that could only mean she was pushing the gas pedal to the floor. She didn't stop or slow down, and barely missed the mailbox and a streetlight. The car was lurching as it went, because it had a manual transmission and Charlotte had never learned to drive a stick shift. Between the grinding gears, lurching motion, erratic steering, and high rate of speed, I knew Charlotte was going to hurt herself or someone else. She had to be stopped. I didn't know what to do, so I called my brother, the attorney. "Call the cops," he said. "She is going to hit someone, and you will be liable!" So, I called the cops.

I explained to dispatch that my wife had taken the car and, though I was sure she would come back with it soon, she wasn't in her right mind and represented a clear danger to herself, other drivers, and even pedestrians. Could they send someone over?

They took that question seriously. Within minutes, eight policeman from the local police department were on the scene, taking my statement and wanting to know if I wanted to press charges against Charlotte for domestic abuse. No, I said, I was only interested in everyone's staying safe, Charlotte included. The police put out an all-points bulletin on my wife. It was a surreal moment for me.

As I was concluding the report in the kitchen with one of the police officers, we heard a squeal of brakes and ran to the window. Around the corner on two wheels came Charlotte in the BMW. She jumped out of the car, red-faced and wild-looking, with her hair sticking out at all angles and her clothes disheveled. She looked like a crazy person, and her actions matched her appearance.

When the police moved to block her from entering the house, she began shrieking at the cops, "Get out of my f—ing way! This is my f—ing house, and I'm going inside! That's my f—ing husband in there."

The police explained that she was to stay out in the front yard and answer some questions about the car and the situation. She was having none of that and began screaming ever louder. The cops tried to calm her, talking softly and slowly, as though to a dangerous animal, and then she turned into one, taking wild swings at the officers and even kicking them. Charlotte made a run for the kitchen, and the cops, taken by surprise by her sudden move, were reduced to following her in as she burst through the kitchen door.

Two officers started wrestling with her as she headed straight for me, and she tried to grab one of the officers' guns. With one well-practiced move, the cops took her down to the ground. Charlotte started bucking wildly and, though she weighed only 95 pounds, she had manic strength, so one police officer knelt on her back and cuffed her. I had a slight moment of insanity then myself. Seeing the policeman lay hands on my wife, I almost reacted out of protective instinct and punched the cop, but the reality of the situation took hold and I stepped back. The officers carried her out, with her cursing all the way, and put her in the back of the police car. Inside the kitchen, we could still hear her screaming.

The officer explained that, since neither party was accusing the other of any physical abuse, a domestic abuse charge was not going to be a part of this event. The police were going file a disorderly person report and have a psych evaluation done on her down at the station. I was advised not to come along. They told me, when I inquired later, that Charlotte had been evaluated and released on her own recognizance. I wasn't sure what that meant for us, but I was soon to find out.

A few days later, my doorbell rang and I went, with Baby Abigail in my arms, to answer it. It was the same police officer who had taken the lead in the BMW incident. "May I come in to speak with you, Mr. Sweetwood?" he asked, clutching a clipboard. "Sure," I replied, and in he came. Right behind him came five more cops—all with guns drawn!

There is one thing good Jewish boys (even those who know nothing about being a good Jewish boy) are, and that is respectful of the law. We don't join street gangs, beat other kids up, or go to jail (except for "financial irregularities"). If West Side Story had been cast with Jews, it would have been just an orchestral piece (you did good, Leonard).

Our respect for authority isn't based in cowardice (though all those Cossacks and pogroms no doubt loom large in our genetic memory); it's just that we like to avoid trouble. "Outthink Them" should be our motto. We are a reasonable race—much less bare-knuckle than "Let's make a deal." But reason seemed to have no place in the current situation.

The lead cop started screaming in my face, but I was too disoriented by the drawn guns to understand any of what he was saying. He kept screaming at me and, frightened, Baby Abigail started to cry very loudly. The noise brought the other kids and the nannies to peer down over the banister of the steps, and soon they began wailing, too. What the cop was saying was, "Put up your hands!"

"How can I put up my hands? I'm holding a baby," I said.

"Put them up now," he yelled, and the guns now were pointed at me.

I was frozen into immobility, and at last one of the nannies came down the stairs and took the baby from me. I raised my arms and kept asking, "What is this about? What is going on?"

The cops finally stopped yelling and answered my questions.

It seems that, after her release, Charlotte had gone back to the police station, showed the cops the bruises on her back and wrists from where they had knelt on her and cuffed her, and claimed I had beaten her up and threatened her life with my .357 Magnum revolver!

Since these were the same cops who had done the kneeling on and cuffing at the BMW incident, they knew what she was saying wasn't true. But they also undoubtedly knew that, if I weren't to blame, they were. They may have blanched at the thought of a future lawsuit, so they swallowed her lie whole and ran with it.

They were armed with a search warrant for any weapons and ammunition and were authorized to take my license to carry a gun and any weapon they found. I did, in fact, have handguns, all of which were secured in an old safe at my place of business. Not only were my dad and brother and I target shooters who collected guns, but our old warehouse had been located in such a dangerous area of Yonkers, New York, that when an alarm went off after midnight, the police wouldn't even bother to investigate it. Taking care of myself when working late in that neighborhood was my own responsibility. Hence the guns at work. I never owned the .357 Magnum of which Charlotte had spoken. With her increasingly erratic behavior, I was worried she might do harm to herself or one of the kids, which was the main reason for not having any guns in the house—even properly stored in a locked box.

I accompanied the police to my new place of business in Scarsdale, New York, and turned over the guns, ammo, and my license. (Good citizen that I was, I was just relieved I would get no points on my license.) Soon after we arrived, the Scarsdale police showed up to claim that my case was theirs, as the guns were on their turf. Listening to the two police departments bicker, I felt as if I were on an episode of CSI.

The cops took the guns, my license to own them, and the purple RAV4 I had bought for the nannies, before letting me go. I went home to my terrified children—ages 18 months through 8 years old.

Restraining orders were issued both to Charlotte and me, saying that she would not come to our home, nor could I come to hers, though I didn't even know its location or that she had moved in with a boyfriend—a police officer boyfriend at that.

I felt like I had fallen down the rabbit hole but plastered an all-too-fake smile on my face and tried to act normal in front of the children. You could cut the tension in the house with a knife, however, and it made for an uneven atmosphere.

Little by little, there was incremental improvement, though. The kids' moods went up and down, just less often and less erratically as days went by. They still mentioned their mommy all the time, asking where she was and when she was coming home, but they seemed to take my falsely cheerful answers of "she's at school" and "she'll be back soon" as sufficient information, until the next time they asked.

But they started to turn to Yael and Shira for most of their comfort and to me for anything with which they needed help. Daddy, can you open this bottle? Daddy, can you hand me down that glass? Daddy, how many stars are there? Daddy, will you be the one to read to me tonight?

I particularly enjoyed telling them a special bedtime story I would make up each night. It had child characters in it whose names coincidentally had the same first letters as those in the first names of my children. Those stories seemed to provide great comfort for them. They kept asking me to tell those stories every night. It felt great to be so wanted by my kids.

I began to feel like I was a bigger part of their lives than just the one who brought home money, and I liked the feeling. On my drives home, I began to notice my shoulders were less hunched, and I looked forward to walking in the house and seeing my children.

All the confusion and upset of Charlotte's storming in and out of the house and our lives had caused the kids' grades in school to slip, and a few minor incidences of their acting out in class put me in touch with the schools' administrators. I had made the schools aware that I would probably be the one with whom they would be dealing should anything arise with the kids—at least for the time being. My wife was away "pursuing her education," "would be back soon," "had left me in temporary charge," and a mouthful of other lies I spouted to avoid confronting the too-painful truth.

I could feel their judgment. I could almost read their thoughts: Where there is smoke, there's fire, they were thinking. He must be a pretty awful man to have his wife run away like that. No mother would leave her children otherwise. I was the victim of reverse discrimination before such a thing even had a title. My kids had felt the judgments and tension too, but things were looking a little less bleak as the days went by.

The kids' grades began to rise now that the nannies and I went over their homework with them every night. Shira, who was very well educated, handled the general subjects, and I was the go-to math and history guy. We'd sit around the table after our family dinners and work out the equations, and in this way, I got to know my kids, really know them, in a way I had never done before. I discovered them as individuals with separate personalities, not just as a group of five but as special people, each with his or her own traits and challenges. Through helping them solve the math problems, I got to learn how their minds worked and how they handled praise and frustration and disappointment.

Learning these things would later help me guide them as young adults, because they didn't change so much as they grew. They only got taller. I've heard it said that you can help mold your kids only until they reach the age of 12 (some say their personalities are pretty set by the age of 2), and after that you really can only help keep them from getting hit by a bus. There might be something to that. Those evenings around the table really helped me gain insight into my children that I had never had before and would have missed if I hadn't had to step up and become a real parent, not just a breadwinner.

But it wasn't all work and no play.

We'd spend weekends together doing simple things—visiting the nearby parks and playgrounds, hitting a matinee movie, piling in the car to go get ice cream (each child had a different favorite, of course). We kicked the ball around in the backyard, played a million games of catch, went Rollerblading and sledding and learned to ice skate. I discovered I had not forgotten how to laugh, and my kids rediscovered how to giggle too. We read books, sang songs, sat the nannies down and cooked dinner for them a few times (wrecking the kitchen in the process), and tried to top each other as to who could tell the stupidest jokes.

   ***

Charlotte had engaged a local attorney, and I was glad she chose him, because he was not the most expensive lawyer she could have gotten and it would be me, as the sole breadwinner, who would be paying her legal fees, as well as mine. Charlotte hadn't had a job or earned a wage since I had met her.

I decided I might need an attorney of my own. The only lawyer I knew came from my company's law firm, which happened to have exactly one lawyer, a nice older lady named Leora who did matrimonial law for some of its clients, and she agreed to take the case.

A date was set shortly thereafter for me to appear in court in White Plains, at the Westchester County Courthouse with my corporate lawyer. I was glad she was an older woman, and I hoped she would be maternal enough to show my wife I wasn't trying to hurt her! I just wanted Charlotte to feel better and stop this nonsense.

I was somewhat intimidated, though. I didn't have much experience with courthouses. When the police made us all step aside at the metal detectors so that a line of prisoners, in orange jumpsuits and shackled together at the ankles, could shuffle through, the sight rattled me.

Charlotte's attorney and mine had a conference about a settlement before we had to stand in front of a judge. My attorney convinced hers that Charlotte did not want to testify over specifics in the case. She would have to confirm under oath facts like dates and where we had both been at the time of the alleged assault, and where the weapon in question actually was and a myriad of other little details. Her lawyer knew she couldn't stand up to rigorous examination about those questions, because Charlotte had already proved a bit shaky in her answers to the questions he had posed about the case. There were contradictions when her answers were held up against the police report, and these made glaring holes in her story.

Because of these inconsistences in her story, Charlotte's attorney realized quickly that her accusations against me were fabricated. He urged her to drop the charges against me and to agree to a consent order. My attorney sat with hers and hammered out a deal that involved my paying her even more money than the several thousand dollars a month I had been giving her to live on since she had moved out.

The judge, coincidentally, turned out to be an old friend of my father's.

He asked me if the kids were all staying with me, and when I said they were, he asked, in a rather incredulous voice, "And you are still okay with paying her money even if she isn't the one taking care of the kids?" (I had been voluntarily giving Charlotte several thousand dollars a month even without a court order. If I hadn't, how would she live? I didn't want her to suffer.)

When I said I was fine with continuing to support her, he rolled his eyes, said okay, and dismissed the charges against me with no adjudication. That meant the charges were dropped as though they hadn't happened— with one exception: a new federal law had kicked in and, because a restraining order had been issued against me, I could no longer own a firearm. It would take me ten years and a case before the Supreme Court to have that right restored to me.

Charlotte had been seeing a psychologist and said she had been "detailing all the abuse." The psychologist asked me to come in and speak to her. She said she was really trying to "dig into Charlotte and get a handle on her mental state." Charlotte gave her psychologist permission to speak freely to me, though she later took that right away. The therapist met with Charlotte every week, and after four or five months delivered the none-too-insightful verdict that Charlotte "had major issues." No kidding.

I was worried about the effect this was having on the children. I had no words for the younger kids to explain their mother's behavior—extra hugs would have to do—but I did speak to the older kids, telling them that their mother was sick and none of this was their fault.

I hoped against hope that things might get a little better now. Charlotte was in therapy. The three older kids were seeing psychiatrists individually, on the advice of my attorney, and at least the kids and their mom would be speaking again.

Her "issues" notwithstanding, the court had ordered supervised visits between Charlotte and the kids, and those needed to be arranged. Embarrassed though I was to ask for help, I did so anyway, tapping my brother, David, to act as supervisor during those visits.

The visits took place at the local Chili's restaurant. The kids would wait impatiently for their mom to arrive, their noses pressed up against the glass, scanning the parking lot. Sometimes they waited in vain and she didn't come at all. Almost always, if she showed up, she was very late and angry and impatient with the kids. She waited until my brother had stepped away to sit in another booth to watch over the proceedings, and then she would bad-mouth me:

"Watch it, kids. Your dad will do to you what he did to me," she'd insist. "He tried to kill me, you know. He'll do the same to you."

As if that weren't frightening enough, she'd harshly whisper, "As soon as they put your father in jail, I'm coming back for all of you."

She packed the destructive power of a hurricane. She confused and frightened the children at each visit, alternating between saying she loved them, she was their mother, they were part of her body, she would never leave them, they were her babies, it was me who was keeping her away, she was lost without them, and telling them they were such awful children that of course, she left them—who would want to take care of such brats?

Aaron had enough of this one day and found his own way out. He asked to go to the bathroom and didn't return for a very long time. My brother wondered if he had been kidnapped or, more likely, as it was 7-year-old Aaron, was busy decorating the bathroom's ceiling with wet toilet paper or doing something equally destructive.

When my brother went to investigate, he found Aaron sitting at the soda bar, surrounded by attentive waitresses, sipping a complimentary milkshake with extra cherries. He had found his own way of not attending the visitation sessions with his mom.

Once the kids and I left only to find she had keyed both sides of our Chevy Suburban, scratching the paint off all the way down the sides. The kids saw the damage and started all yelling at once.

Ethan shrieked, "Mommy did that to the car!" And seeing how upset they were, I felt as embarrassed as though I had done the deed.

I quickly reassured them that we'd get the car fixed immediately. I hadn't yet learned that it was okay for kids to feel pain or outrage or be upset about a situation. I was still in full protect-them-at-all-costs mode.

At the time, the kids and I never spoke about these visits after they were over. It was as though there were an unspoken agreement not to rub salt in our wounds. We had taken our medicine for the week, and now it was over and we were safe again.

The visits soon stopped anyway. Charlotte's cop boyfriend had started driving her to the visits and waiting in the Chili's parking lot until she was done. A few times, we'd see them in the car, circling the parking lot, and they would drive away, with her never coming in at all.

Still, it wasn't enough for me. Charlotte's psychologist asked me to come in and speak with her and Charlotte, and I did. I clung to the secret hope that since she was seeing a professional, Charlotte would get better and we could put the family back together again.

I was awash in a sea of denial.

Eventually, it became impossible to keep repeating that lie to myself and keep my head above water.

When Charlotte accused me of trying to kill her for the umpteenth time, finally something in me snapped. I saw clearly that she was crazy, would always be crazy, and was never going to get any better. My pretty dream of us all becoming a happy family was just that...a dream...a total fantasy and, though it hurt like hell to let that dream die, I had to do so or risk ruining my future and that of my children as well.

One morning, when I looked at the man in the mirror as I shaved, I found myself asking, "Are you really doing the best you can for your kids? How about yourself?" and I knew it was soon going to be time to face reality.

Charlotte wasn't coming back. Our marriage wasn't going through a rough patch. Things weren't going to get better between us. Our marriage was dead, and I needed to get on with its burial. The thought of severing the last thread of hope brought bitter bile to the back of my throat. I felt drained, beaten, and impotent, but one tiny voice of clarity spoke out of the darkness: You will get to the other side of this. Begin now. It is time.

I knew I had to summon up the necessary courage to act, and I did. I finally filed for divorce in August of 1997.

When I told my attorney my decision to finally file for divorce, she said she was relieved and very happy. She had believed all along that was what I should do, but she needed me to reach that conclusion on my own.

But I wasn't free of the storm yet. Charlotte would bring her hurricane force back into our lives once again, via the legal system she had learned to play like a fiddle.

Charlotte's next in a series of high-powered attorneys balked at her continual motions set up just to squeeze me for money, and she fired him. She hired new, more demanding lawyers. A judge would render a decision, and he would tell her lawyer to write it up. Charlotte's attorneys would do so, but add things preferential to their case to it, and the judge would sign the altered document without rereading it. (Proof of this was found in the court reporter's notes when all was settled.)

This whole series of events—psychiatrist's visits, psychologist's visits, lawyers' consultations, motions being written and contested, the whole circus—was bankrupting me, but I would have to live with the circumstances. They weren't new to me.

By the end of September of 1997, Charlotte and I were once again before a judge, and this time it was in divorce court.

Though New York is a no-fault state, grounds were still required, so I cited abandonment and asked for full legal and physical custody of the children. Charlotte's answer finally came when she changed attorneys (again). Now she had engaged the most expensive matrimonial firm in New

York, the firm that had handled Donald Trump's gold-plated divorce. I gritted my teeth about the future bills, but was done being angry and fearful and just wanted to get on with my life.

The court awarded me 100 percent residential custody. That meant Charlotte did not have to sign her parental rights away. All regular day-to-day decisions about the children (school, pediatricians, and so forth) would be made by me, but anything extraordinary, like surgery, she would have to be notified of. If I died, she'd get the kids. (I vowed then and there to get healthier and live a good, long time.) So far, so good, I was thinking as I heard these terms.

The court, at the recommendation of a court-appointed psychologist, ruled that Charlotte be "reintroduced to the children and earn back regular visitation with them." The judge was keen on these visits, saying he wanted to hear reports of her "reintroduction to her children." He believed in a mother's love. If only Charlotte had.

It turned out that there was a social worker (working under the direction of the psychologist, who was now convinced Charlotte had been an abused wife and that I was a monster), who urged her to sue for visitation rights— as a prelude toward gaining custody (and even more of my money).

It was this mental health professional, whom the children had been ordered to see, who said to kids at one session, "Maybe your father really did beat your mother." That statement was enough for Ethan, who jumped up, said his mother was a liar for saying things like that about his father, and walked out. He refused to ever meet with that social worker again.

The court ruled that Charlotte needed to submit to supervised visits at first and then, by adhering to a schedule of consultations with the mental health professionals appointed by the court, could work her way to unsupervised visits.

I was very unhappy about this idea, knowing what having time alone with Charlotte would do to the kids, but I couldn't go against the court order.

Charlotte was directed to stop bad-mouthing me to the children and to spend her few hours a week rebuilding her relationship with the kids. The visits were held at Charlotte's rental home—about five miles from where I was living with the kids. The kids weren't wild about going on that merry-go-round ride again.

After seesawing between terror and joy as they reacted to their mother and her lightning-fast mood changes during the first round of visitations supervised by my brother at Chili's, they had been given a respite when Charlotte stopped showing up for those supervised visits. All of us had seemed to take our first deep breaths in a long time, and now, it seemed, we were to go back to holding our breath again. At least this time, we had fewer expectations. Good thing.□

CHAPTER 6
IT'S ALWAYS DARKEST

Things at home were settling down a bit.

Thanks to the nannies, the children seemed to have learned to take Charlotte's outbursts, threats, and unreliability with a child-sized grain of salt. It seems Yael and Shira were doing what I had been unable to do—explain in some sort of age-appropriate way that Mommy didn't really mean what she said, or that she was just being silly, or that Mommy was the one who was confused. Whatever they said, and however they said it, it seemed to help.

I, their daddy, was too confused to really explain Charlotte's actions in a way that made the kids feel safe, but those nannies did it for me.

"Your daddy will never leave you, and he won't let anyone hurt you," they repeated to each kid in turn, and the children believed them.

Those reassurances seemed to give the kids the armor they needed to protect themselves against Charlotte's sharpest barbs—another type of blanket those young Israeli women provided. They wrapped my kids up, and I will forever be grateful.

***

Another sign that things were calming down in our household and getting better between my kids and myself was the fact that they started hugging me again. All of them were huggers, the boys only slightly less than the girls, and they had all gotten physically close with the nannies right away.

In earlier days, I remember them with their mother—when they were watching TV, when she sang them to sleep with her guitar, after nightmares when they came to our bed to "visit," but all that closeness stopped as Charlotte began withdrawing from them and acting hostile, paranoid, and violent.

Torn between their intrinsic natures—kids who enjoyed a good hug—and being halfway sold on the idea that I might actually hurt them, as was being peddled by their mother in her sickest fantasies, they had pulled back from me. But during this time of trial, the hugs came back. It started with the little ones—quick hugs around my knees, or Baby Abigail throwing her arms around my neck—to even an occasional hug from Lauren or a half-hearted one from Aaron when I let him out of the car at practice. I took them where I could get them and started to look forward to them. Affection from my kids made things look less bleak.

***

Not all was rosy, however. Aaron, particularly, was struggling with school. I wasn't too surprised when I got a call from Aaron's principal. He called me into his office, which had a window overlooking the sports field, to talk about my son, who had been underachieving, to put it mildly.

"Aaron hasn't been doing well," said Principal Henderson, "and I have been watching him. I think he is a very smart kid and has just been laboring about under his situation at home." (So much for my thinking I was keeping our domestic situation a big secret.)

He continued, "I was a troubled kid myself, and one of the things that saved me was soccer, so I suggested that Aaron might want to give that sport a try."

Aaron, a soccer player? Even though Aaron was a very coordinated and athletic kid, the thought had never occurred to me, and I started to say so when the principal directed my attention to the window.

"Look there," he said. "That's Aaron." I looked out the window to see my silent, whirling dervish son dribble down the field like a pro—the black and white of the soccer ball spinning so fast it was hard for the eye to follow, as he feinted around and through the legs of the other players on the field.

"Wow, he's good," I said, quite surprised. "I never knew."

"Yes, he is," said the principal.

I was already clued in to the fact that Aaron needed to be run every day like a thoroughbred horse, or else his manic energy would drive him (and everyone else) crazy. His teachers and several counselors had strongly suggested I put him on the latest form of ADHD meds, which were becoming all the rage. There was no way I was putting my third-grader on drugs, so I had been devising energy-burning activities for him after school and at home.

When the principal spoke to me about soccer, the light dawned. Daily practice would ensure he had to run at least five miles a day, and being on a team would force him to socialize, which would help with his communication problems.

Like every red-blooded American father, my heart swelled with pride at the fantasy that my son might someday be playing in the "big leagues," but I never realized that soccer might be the thing that literally would save my son's life. I also didn't know it would be what would bring us close together for all the rest of his growing-up years, as I drove him to practices and attended his games. I would always be cheering for him and encouraging him, as soccer gave him a way to rise above his circumstances and shift his attention away from his screwed-up home life.

But then my conversation with the principal took another unexpected turn—a more personal one.

The principal said, "I don't know what is going on in your home, just that something is. Why don't you tell me about your situation?"

I was embarrassed and didn't know quite what to say, but there didn't seem to be any easy way for me to avoid answering such a direct question. So, I sketched out for him a bit about what was going on, without bad-mouthing my wife, and he asked, "So, you now are the only one at home raising these kids?"

When he put it that baldly, I had to answer, "Yes, just me and the nannies"

What he said next is what chipped away at my thinking about the situation:

"Good," he said. "Those kids are better off with you and without her."

That thought had never occurred to me. It gave me something to ponder that night and for many nights to come.
***

Charlotte, as should surprise no one by now, kept up her good behavior during visitation with the kids for about as long as it took me to type this sentence. Barely had the kids taken seats in her living room than she was spewing hatred and fear all over them.

Charlotte started in on me again the second she opened her mouth:

"He's an evil man, your father," she hissed, and when Lauren protested that it wasn't true and she loved her dad, Charlotte whirled on her.

"If you don't love me, if none of you love me and you are going to side against me, I am never coming home. You'll never have a mother." She spat out the words like nails. "You don't get to have a mother, because you are terrible children. You are so awful that it is your fault that I had to leave in the first place. Now you are stuck with your father, and you better watch out. Your father will kill you in your sleep."

It wasn't only Charlotte's words that upset the kids though. Their mother, the one who wouldn't return to them, was visibly pregnant with another baby. The older kids noticed, and I was left to explain that they shouldn't take it personally that their mom was having another baby rather than coming home to them. It had nothing to do with their being worthy or lovable. They were both those things and would always be so to me. That was really all I could do.

Soon enough, though, Charlotte stopped showing up for the visits. There was no word of why she stopped appearing. She just didn't come to get them for one visit and then didn't come for the next, until the visits petered out entirely. I drove them to her house and waited in the car while they knocked on her door. No one answered. The kids got back in the car and we went back home. No more visits occurred. Charlotte never asked to see them again—ever—and I thought I saw a tiny light at the end of a long, black tunnel.

Once again, though, I was left trying to explain such behavior to my kids, but I could see that even at their young ages, they, in their own ways, had chalked up her behavior to "that's just the way Mommy is." The nannies and I tried our best to reassure them that it wasn't their fault, that nothing they did or didn't do had caused Mommy to not see them anymore. We spent extra time with each child, much of it with our arms around them, whenever they'd allow such affection. On our side, we were all doing the best we could.

On Charlotte's side, she was up to her old tricks.

Charlotte and her latest lawyers, who I felt were scums of the earth, appealed again, asking for even more money. In order to bolster their case, they filed motion after motion, claiming I beat the kids, misrepresenting previous orders and agreements—every dirty trick in the book to take up time and boost their billable hours.

One of her lawyers even followed me into the men's room and threatened me while I was answering the call of nature. I found the cojones to tell him he'd better get out of there fast, because when I was done, only one of us was going to leave that men's room, and it was going to be me. My frustration knew no bounds.

Not only was I saddled with Charlotte's legal and therapy fees, on top of those for the kids, but Charlotte continued to level wild accusations at me at every opportunity, all couched in legalese that made her sound reasonable.

She won every ridiculous motion—including one that said I didn't pay her monthly support check. We submitted a copy of the canceled check to the court. That evidence was disregarded, and I had to pay again. She grew emboldened. We appeared before the same judge every time. Charlotte would cry and ka-ching: motion granted.

Finally, we got another judge, and this one didn't even read the paperwork. He looked at me and said, "Pay up or go to jail."

The final divorce decree was issued on March 22, 2001. I was technically "free," but my nightmare was just beginning.

I was ordered to pay all legal and expert fees, now amounting to hundreds of thousands of dollars, as well as give her equitable distribution equal to one-third of my share of my business, equivalent to $2 million, payable at 7.5 percent interest for 20 years, tax-free. In addition, I was ordered to per her alimony of $100,000 a year for two years and $80,000 a year for life after that—and I was only 37 years old!

The agreement also stated that if the business ever became more profitable, she could ask for more money at any time. If I sold the business, the remainder of the entire $2 million would come due immediately, and bankruptcy could not discharge the debt I owed her.

Attorneys I knew said it was the worst divorce decree they had ever seen.

I would be paying her more than 100 percent of my income for the rest of my life, and I still had kids to raise. Now I would have no money to do so. She would have none of the responsibility for the children, but would take all the money necessary for their care.

I appealed, but it took another year to reach the appellate court, and they remanded the case back to the original judge, who was none too pleased to have his judgment overturned.

He changed only part of the agreement, that of the amount of alimony. The judge lowered the alimony from $80,000 to $43,000 (still for life), leaving the rest of the agreement in place. On top of the $7,000 equitable distribution per month I was paying, I was also shelling out another $8,000 a month to clear the second payment of $100,000 per year I owed (having already paid the first $100,000).

The judge had basically given all the working capital of the business and all its future profits to Charlotte.

This latest round of appeals had elicited a furious backlash from the New York appellate court, which informed us that ours was the longest divorce case in state history and we should cease and desist. "Go away," is what they said, and the agreement stood.

I sold our house and moved into a dump, one without even a bathroom that didn't have leaks, drips and cracks, to keep the kids in the same school district. Then I borrowed more money—from banks, credit cards, and my mom, and I put my head down to work ever harder to try to raise enough money to meet this new, horrifying obligation. I felt like an ox lashed to a plow, heavily burdened, barely able to lift my legs for each new step, but determined to survive.

I was devastated financially and, as my doctor said, looked like a patient with terminal cancer. That wasn't far from the truth. I had a lifelong illness—that of being yoked to this woman—and it just might kill me.

CHAPTER 7
NOT THE ABCS

"You, who are on the road, must have a code that you can live by." So sings David Crosby (though surviving such a harrowing drug addiction, he probably could have used a better road map himself).

For me, I would have happily bought any book that would have given me such a code, one that told me how to parent, but there is no such thing. Dr. Phil can tell you to share breakfast with your family every day to hash out any potential problems, Amy Chua can admonish us all to be Tiger Moms, and Supernanny can stop the tantrums of the brattiest kids with a rewards chart, but when it comes to the real world, kids don't follow the program.

There is no program for parenting.

There is only developing intuition, recognizing when you've got it, and then making good guesses. It's like guerrilla marketing. If your company's business plan isn't working, you ditch the business plan. If something isn't working with your child, you spin again.

I had a lot to learn and luckily, with all those kids, I had plenty of opportunities to practice. It is good to have a whole slew of kids, I found, because I got to spread out the screw-ups. Nobody got the full weight of my half-baked parenting attempts.

Though we had been getting better (and closer together as a family), once Charlotte had truly moved out and the endless court proceedings began, not only did my level of anxiety increase, but so did that of my children.

Emily began weeping again. She took it particularly hard that her mommy was gone for good. The only way she would see her was if Charlotte ever attended the court- ordered sessions and, even at that, the version of Mommy she got there didn't help fill the hole ripped in her heart.

Before the courts got involved and Charlotte kept some of her most bizarre behavior under wraps, she had told the kids they could no longer call her Mommy, saying that was because such terrible children "didn't deserve a mommy." She then informed them that they could call her

Charlotte or, preferably, Captain, after Star Trek's Captain Kirk. When the kids slipped and called her Mommy, she would lash out at them, enraged they had disobeyed her orders. (They never did call her Captain, but her insistence that they do certainly did confuse them, and Emily responded to confusion with big, silent tears that just coursed down her cheeks. It broke my heart to see them.)

Lauren was more dramatic in her displeasure. I came home once at Yael's request because she couldn't talk Lauren out of a very dangerous course of action. Lauren had climbed out her bedroom window and up over the roof gable, and was lying out on the slate roof, close to falling to the ground far below. I had to literally talk her off the ledge; though I am fairly sure she wasn't consciously choosing to commit suicide, she was taking her life in her hands. Crying as hard as she was, she could barely see to come back in through the window. I used a voice as soft and gentle as I would have if I were dealing with a wild animal—and that description wasn't so far off the mark. Lauren didn't recover from her trauma about her mother right away, but from then on confined herself to continued pubescent defiance.

I understood Lauren's running to the roof. Sometimes I, too, wanted to get away from it all and felt the house couldn't contain my grief.

The boys got in some trouble at school, and nail biting and bedwetting hit an uptick at home as Charlotte and I went at each other with lawyers and summonses and in court. Even Baby Abigail felt the tension in the air and was becoming particularly fretful. Yael and Shira never batted an eye throughout this, however, reminding me by their calm presence and their unshakable routines that "this too shall pass."

All the kids were going to shrinks during this time, and perhaps it helped them (though I am unsold on the belief that play therapy for little ones does any good). The older kids didn't want to go, and I, who had to attend family therapy with them, wasn't too crazy about the idea either. It wasn't just the expense—though that was a factor. I was being squeezed dry of every nickel by Charlotte, and the whole family was feeling the pinch. It wasn't as though we didn't have a roof over our heads or food on our table, but I was certainly preoccupied and distracted with my constant need to generate money. There was never enough, and we lived paycheck to paycheck, and I was worried that I wasn't giving my children the attention they needed and deserved. I was carrying the weight of such responsibility on my shoulders, I wasn't sure I was being a good parent.

One of the mental health professionals (one who had been appointed by the court) further opened my eyes about our situation, in much the same way as Aaron's high school principal had done.

"Matt, I want you to look at your situation this way," he said. "Right now, you and the kids are inside a castle with the drawbridge pulled up tight. Charlotte is on the outside. All of you are safe on the inside. Keep it that way. You and your children are much better off without that woman in your lives."

I was still a little surprised by that sentiment. I had a lot of trouble rearranging my belief system to say that I, as the father, not only had a right and responsibility to raise my kids myself, but that I might be better at parenting than a woman. Given the way I had been raised, that was quite a concept.

For the kids' part, the scattered visits with their mother, when she was still showing up for such visits, confused them at first. They wanted to see her but never knew which person they were going to get —Mommy or the Captain. Would she be yelling, nasty, crying, or happy to see them?

One thing that was consistent about each visit was that, sometime during it, Charlotte would begin complaining about me. Often, she would tell the kids lurid tales about what I did to her or would do to them, and the older kids struggled about whether or not there was any truth to what she was saying. Was I really a monster who hurt their mom and who would hurt them? My brother, who had agreed to act as the supervisor at those earlier supervised visits the children had with their mother at Chili's, clued me in to what she was saying at the meetings and how poison was being poured into their ears. Ethan was the one who first walked out of a meeting with his mother when she was bad-mouthing me, saying he didn't believe a word she was saying and telling me he wouldn't go back to another visit with her. Loyal to the core is Ethan.

But loyalty to me is one thing, and it has little to do with their behavior to outsiders. There was a period when the older kids acted bad and disrespectfully toward others, and I wasn't quite sure how to handle it. I had to learn another lesson about parenting.

At first, I saw how the kids were acting and, though I was disappointed by it, I felt I understood it. Poor kids, I thought. Look at all they've been through. Rejected by their mother, even abandoned by her; no wonder they are acting like they do. And I felt very sorry for them. I was to learn that pity is as corrosive as battery acid, and pity for kids is no better for them than self-pity was for me. When I saw the effect such pity had on them, I decided (with great trepidation) to try another way.

What if I was harder on them and expected them to overcome their circumstances, to act like people instead of objects of pity? What would happen if I didn't kowtow to their whims, but instead expected them to rise to the occasion and act with respect for themselves, me, and others?

I didn't know if that would work, but I felt it couldn't hurt, so I gave it a whirl. I insisted they talk to me in a normal voice (no yelling at me), and I did the same with them. I made them sit down to look me in the eye and have a real conversation about what was troubling them. I asked them questions that couldn't be answered with a grudging yes or no. I discovered that really listening to another person (even a kid) is the greatest compliment. We talked things over, and when they wouldn't and acted out again, they were sent to time-out (or, as they got older, grounded) until they could act better (no more smacking them). I accepted no excuses and didn't give in to feeling sorry for them. This was the hand life had dealt them (and me), and we'd have to learn to function under the circumstances in which we found ourselves. Whining was out.

I began to have expectations for them, and I trusted they would meet them. After an initial period of griping and grousing, they did just that. I learned by doing this that kids, though they are precious, are not fragile. They don't break with normal handling, and they appreciated the structure I insisted upon. It made them feel safe to have someone other than themselves in charge.

The tantrums faded away. The crying jags stopped. The bed linens stayed dry and the cuticles intact. They started to treat me, and one another, with greater respect, and we reached a level of harmony in our home I never thought possible.

Another thought had occurred to me: By sheltering my kids from every bump and pothole in the road, I was crippling them. How would they learn that they could handle such things in their own lives if they weren't given a chance to overcome their troubles as they cropped up? I wouldn't always be there to shelter them, and life, as I knew all too well, wasn't always easy and never went as planned. By insisting they get control of their own feelings and keep going despite them, I was—as that old adage goes—not just giving them a fish, thus stopping their hunger for a day, but teaching them to fish so they could spend a lifetime feeding themselves.

I changed my thinking about my own role too. It happened like a flash of inspiration from on high, smack in the middle of a most unlikely setting—Chuck E. Cheese's. That chaotic madhouse of animatronic lunacy was a warehouse for bad kid behavior. That asylum of pinball machines, video games, ball pits, and a robotic stage show hosted by a giant mouse was the place for kids' birthday parties. I went to dozens of them there. But one day, amidst the leftover rubbery pizza crusts, my elbows stuck to the table in puddles of spilled soda, my feet glued to the floor by some unidentified grosser substance, it hit me.

I looked around at the gossiping, mean-mouthed mothers who had been shooting me hostile sidelong glances because I was a male and therefore totally out of place at that den of matronly iniquity (any self-respecting man would be home watching the game), and I realized what I had been doing wrong. In my attempt to spare my poor motherless children any pain, I had been trying to maintain the status quo of their lives and doing what Charlotte would have done had she been there in her normal role. I was trying to be a mother, the one thing I could never be! Right then and there, I vowed to never visit a Chuck E. Cheese's again (or a McDonald's PlayPlace or anywhere else the herd of mothers corralled their children so they could bitch about nail salons or talk trash about one of their number who wasn't there that day). Enough! I was going to be a father. I went out and immediately bought season tickets for all of us to the New Jersey Devils hockey games and taught them all to enjoy ice hockey. (Now those games are a family tradition and, even though the kids are adults, whenever we are together we head for the arena to cheer on our team.)

Once I stepped beyond my paralyzing anxiety about making decisions, I discovered I had good instincts. I might not have known squat about being a parent, but I was capable of learning and had more untapped resources than I knew. I would learn later that these resources are actually bottomless, and I can cope with anything with enough spiritual help.

On that note, I was getting spiritual help and didn't know it. Remember the mezuzah Shira had insisted I put on the front-door lintel? Well, one evening the bell rang and when I answered it, I found an Orthodox Jewish man—yarmulke, payos (side curls), and all—holding the hand of a little girl. "We came to say thank you, Mr. Sweetwood," the man said, "for all the clothing and goods you donated to the struggling young families from my synagogue. I am Rabbi Herzog, and Yael told me what you had done. When my daughter, Ava," he said, nodding to the little girl at his side, "was a little fearful of ringing the bell of such a big house, I told her not to be afraid. I pointed out the mezuzah and told her that meant we were at the house of

Leader of the Pack

friend."

I told the rabbi he was very welcome for the donations, but when he asked, "May I invite you to come to services at our Chabad synagogue?" I thanked him for his invitation but demurred. Religion? Not for me.

That was another part of myself of which I was ignorant. As the rabbi had told his little girl, I was a friend of that synagogue and the people who attended. I just hadn't met them yet. I was also being watched over by a higher power, who was blessing our home and me personally, though I hadn't met Him yet either.

One of the first divine gifts I received was a clearing of the mind. I was peeling away years of fear, negativity, and self-doubt, like the layers of an onion, to reveal the man inside. I was learning that there was more to me than I thought there was, and I was as capable of being a good parent as anyone else, even the supposed experts. I was also discovering I wasn't just a good parent but a good person. I was learning what type of man I was, and I was finding a way to stand tall again.

As I discovered more about myself in this way, I could more clearly see my kids too.

Lauren was the leader of the pack. The other kids turned to her when something went wrong in their circle. It was like Downton Abbey—the grownups (the nannies and I), were one society upstairs, and an entirely different society existed downstairs. The kids communicated to one another with some sort of unspoken telepathy, and all of them deferred to Lauren. She was a "little mother," and so I allowed her extra responsibility in the house and for the younger kids. I asked her advice about what was going on with the rest of the children, and she blossomed. We established a level of communication we keep to this day, and I still value her opinion about the others (who continue to confide in her).

Emily needed encouragement and praise, and I began to seek out things she did well so that I could heap compliments upon her. She, too, turned like a flower to the sun, and the weeping slowed to a trickle.

Ethan was contentious; he has been a fighter since birth. Rather than engage his talents in constant arguments, I found things we could agree upon. I admitted he might be right in any opposing stance he took (who can argue when your adversary is admitting you are right?). Then I taught him to wrestle and brought him to karate. He learned to direct his anger in constructive ways. We also wrestled on the floor and tried to beat each other at arm-wrestling. I grabbed Aaron and threw him into our pileups and let both boys get physical with me to help them work out their churning emotions.

This new awareness of who my children really were wasn't foolproof. Aaron literally barely spoke to anyone until he was out of high school, but his grades began going up (slightly), he was proving to be a soccer star, and he seemed less troubled.

Abigail and Emily were the children I got to raise as mine almost from birth, and they both loved me wholeheartedly. All I had to do was love them wholeheartedly right back. I had to overcome my own fear and trepidation about everything going wrong in my life long enough to admit into my heart the pure, raw beam of love from my baby girl. Even in adulthood, Abigail is the most attentive and Emily is the most overtly loving of my children. Their love was a balm to my own troubled spirit while I was learning how to parent.

There was a lot I didn't know and there were many situations I didn't have a clue how to handle over the years—puberty pains, menstrual periods, cystic acne, teenage romance, academic failures, adolescent drama—but then again, no child comes with an owner's manual of what to do in every situation. I learned by trial and error—just like everyone else learns.

Through this time my kids also taught me the most valuable of lessons: everyone deserves to be loved. Everyone. Even me. Though I felt lower than an earthworm and any self-esteem I had was shattered by my wife's treatment of me, my children taught me even I was worthy of love.

That was a lesson worth all the pain.□

CHAPTER 8
DO AS I SAY, NOT AS I DO

People came out of the woodwork with lots to say. As if a dad with five kids under his care can't survive without their input. Mothers, always mothers (my male acquaintances just shook their head at my stories, clapped my shoulder, and cracked open another beer), offered unsolicited and usually useless advice:

"You should ground those kids to make them study. Lock them in their room and no TV till their grades go up."

"Tell Aaron he doesn't get to eat until he asks for the food out loud. That'll get him talking."

"If Emily were my kid, if she didn't cut it out, I'd give her something to cry about."

"My kids never had that problem, but if they had, here's what I would have done…"

"Have you thought about boarding school?"

"Those kids should be medicated."

"You should try to reconcile with your wife."

And always, the inevitable, "You should get married again."

Mind you, none of these people ever shared my experience. Hell, hardly anyone anywhere had shared my experience, but I found that, while my facts might be different, my feelings were shared by single parents, of both genders, everywhere. But that connection was far in the future. First I had to deal with the present moment and the endless cacophony of voices that surrounded me.

Everybody, it seemed, had an opinion.

My mom couldn't believe at first that Charlotte had just got up and left her own children. Despite the fact that she had never particularly liked Charlotte, the thought of a mother—any mother—doing that was shocking to my mom. She had always thought Charlotte was lazy, mostly I think because Charlotte didn't work outside the home, and that was a totally alien concept to my hard-working, old-school mom.

My mother also didn't understand, after having held down roles as homemaker and business owner (for 50 years) at the same time, what Charlotte did all day, since the house and kids were so visibly neglected.

True, my mother had been kept from having the closest of relationships with my kids, her grandchildren, because of Charlotte's weird prohibition of my family's coming near "her" kids, but my mother did have eyes. She also saw how terribly unhappy I was, though I didn't complain to her about my wife out of a strange sense of loyalty to Charlotte. If I look back on the situation truthfully, I was invested in the role of martyr I adopted to feed my self-pity. (Poor me, all alone, no one to share my burdens with…you get the picture.) No mother, even one who had been as distracted as mine growing up, likes to see her child abused. I was, and my mother saw it. If, in fact, there was any silver lining about our desperate situation, it was that my mother got to step in, offer help, and grow closer to my kids. With Charlotte gone and money beyond tight, my mother, despite severe health problems of her own, pitched in when she could with childcare and certainly opened her wallet and heart to us.

My brother, with whom I had not been particularly close since childhood, also stepped up. Accepting the job of supervisor at all of Charlotte's supervised visits, he observed (and was often personally splattered with) the muck that was raised by Charlotte when she was being her most disgusting. During her visits, she often hurled invectives at him too, and I owe him a debt for sitting there and taking it all for the sake of myself and my children. He went above and beyond the "good uncle" title and proved himself a great brother.

As with any situation that provides great fodder for gossip, our family was the talk of the town. I couldn't go the grocery store or post office without running into one of the "well-meaning" people who said they had heard about my "terrible situation and would be happy to help." They wouldn't, of course, have been happy to help, but they were delighted to offer their opinions. Since these were based on fragments of information (and those fragments were usually wrong), their opinions weren't worth anything.

My situation, as the single father of five, was unheard of at the time (and is pretty rare even now), but like it or not, I was going to hear their solution to my problems. They told me what they had done to straighten out their kid, or what they had heard about people who weren't there to defend themselves against some gossipy character assassination, or how they had seen a program on TV dealing with something like what I was dealing with at home. Then they would judge, moralize, dispense advice like they were the Most High, repeat it to make sure even someone as slow-witted as I could remember it, and saunter off to go talk about me behind my back.

The gist of most backstabbing conversations about my situation was that where there is smoke, there is fire. If a mother left her children, there surely was some nefarious act committed by the father to force her to go. Otherwise, it was unthinkable. A mother would never leave her children! No mother was that unnatural. In our case, it must be that I beat or tortured Charlotte, that poor woman, then forced her from our happy home, and turned her own children against her. What kind of beast was I? the prosecuting gossipers would ask. I was tried, convicted, and sentenced to hang without a chance to even hear, much less defend myself against, those accusations.

I didn't even really understand this was happening until some families in town refused to let their kids play with my kids. Then my children started telling me that their former friends were shunning them like they were outcast Amish. I got used to the malicious attacks disguised as helping hands from acquaintances and neighbors, but was a bit taken aback when I got a call from one of the kids' teachers.

"Mr. Sweetwood, this is Jan Jenkins, one of Emily's teachers."

"Yes, Mrs. Jenkins, what can I do for you?" I said.

"Well, I wanted you to know that I think Emily isn't being cared for properly at home," she announced.

"What?"

"Yes, I think her choice of clothes are ugly, and I don't care for the nutritional level of the lunch she has brought to school. I understand your wife is gone and left you in charge of the children. I'm calling to tell you I don't think you are doing a very good job of caring for them, if Emily is any indication. If I were her mother…"

I can barely tell you my feelings upon receiving this phone call. It is a mark that I was recovering, I think, when I didn't take this nasty criticism, agree with it, and curl up into a ball of shame and humiliation. Instead, I saw red. I got so angry, I almost punched a wall.

"Well, Ms. Jenkins, you are not Emily's mother and I am Emily's father, so how my child is dressed or her lunch is none of your business! I take good care of my children, better care than most other parents take care of theirs, and in much tougher circumstances. So, the next time you feel like butting your judgmental nose into somebody's business, go find another family to bother. Oh, and one more thing, Ms. Jenkins, I do not give you permission to examine Emily's lunch or anything else without my permission. Am I being clear?!"

And I hung up the phone.

Maybe I had crossed some Rubicon about getting pushed around by women, but whatever it was, I felt good having stood up for myself. Instead of taking every body shot anyone threw, I was learning to fight back, to man up by standing up for myself and my children.

But, proving the adage "One step forward and two steps back," my newfound ballsiness was about to be tested.

Charlotte began making accusations against me to the Department of Family Services, who informed the school of her allegations. The school nurses started taking my kids out of class to check them for signs of abuse. Next the DFS would show up at the door of our home and tell the nannies to fetch Emily. When Emily was presented, the DFS agents would have her raise her shirt to look for nonexistent bruising on her back and ribs. It was frightening to the child and humiliating to me, yet I was powerless to stop it. I was also terrified that the kids would be taken away from me and, since Charlotte was obviously an unfit mother, what would happen if my children were removed from my care? Would they end up in foster homes? I knew enough about the system to know that once that happened, we would never be free of that horrific government oversight. Chopping off any of the tentacles of that octopus would only mean another would grow in its place.

Also, I was about to undergo another, more insidious, test regarding backstabbers.

As I said, I didn't have many friends to rely upon, but I had become friendly with a couple who lived on the other side of town. Margaret and Bob Klein were a long-married couple with several children who were around the ages of my kids, and the children had become playmates. At first, the kids would play in the street or the yards of our respective houses, but soon they were hanging at each other's houses, playing video games and generally getting underfoot.

Margaret never seemed to mind adopting my herd of kids. She came from a big family, and as she said, "Once you get such a crowd, it doesn't matter if you add a few more to the mix." She was an easygoing, laid-back type of mom, and I welcomed her help.

"Please, Matt, think nothing of it. The kids are running all over the yard either way. The more, the merrier," she said.

"I'd be happy to drive them to practice," Margaret would offer. "I'm passing by your side of town with my kids anyway."

"I'll just throw a few more hotdogs on the grill. A few more mouths to feed doesn't matter around this place," Margaret would say, laughing.

"Matt, I know what you are going through," Margaret said one evening. "Nobody should have to carry such a burden alone. I want you to know I am here for whatever you need. I am happy to help in any way."

She was sort of a maternal angel to my motherless children, I thought. How lucky we were to have such a great neighbor and good friend.

My kids were spending even more time over at the Kleins' house: sleepovers, barbecues, and even going over there a couple of times a week for dinner. When Margaret asked if they could take Lauren and Aaron on vacation to the lake house the Kleins had at the Long Island Shore, I said yes. Actually, I was relieved that at least some of the kids' care was off my hands for a while, and I knew they'd be fine. Margaret was a good mother. (Her husband wouldn't say "boo" to a mouse, but he seemed like an amiable guy, if somewhat overly devoted to watching golf on TV.)

So, the kids went to the shore house with the Klein family and, after that, Margaret started showing up at our house more often. I'd come back from work to find her in our kitchen, talking to Yael about recipes. Soon she started bringing baked goods over.

"Lauren says you like apple pie," Margaret would say as I walked in the kitchen.

"I am a sucker for homemade apple pie," I'd reply smiling and, accepting a hearty slice, would begin digging in.

But, when Margaret started to discuss Aaron's grades on a recent test with me, I started to feel a slight warning sensation, like a little blip in the Force—Margaret seemed to be stepping over the line of good neighbor or even intimate friend, but I dismissed my feeling as an overreaction. (I was still smarting from that teacher's call.)

Yael had sensed the same thing but had an explanation for Margaret's behavior. "She likes you, Mr. Matt. You know, like a woman likes a man."

"Don't be silly, Yael," I said. "Margaret and Bob have been married almost 20 years. I mean, she's got to be in her mid-40s or so." (Someone in their mid-40s seemed as ancient as the Crypt Keeper to me at that time. I was in my mid-30s, and I guess I thought people lost interest in sex and romance after 45.) "You are imagining things."

"We shall see, Mr. Matt," said Yael, with the "I know everything and you know nothing" smirk I'd seen on her face before. Then I dismissed the conversation from my overly busy brain.

To celebrate the end of school, our family decided to have a backyard barbecue, and the kids got to invite all their friends' families. Of course, the guest list included Margaret, Bob, and their brood.

It also included a woman who was one of my first experimental forays back into the dating world (more to come about those days). The relationship was brand new and not very serious yet, but I thought it might be a nice way to introduce her to my kids and my kids to her without making a big deal about it to either side. She was a slim and pretty woman in her late 20s, pleasant and amiable to the kids and all the other guests at the party.

Everyone was milling around the yard and through the house, and Yael and Shira were helping organize the food in the kitchen, when in slammed Margaret. "Slammed" is a carefully chosen word, since her appearance probably wouldn't have been noted in the hustle and bustle if she hadn't banged down a casserole dish so hard on the counter, Yael stopped what she was chopping to see it had broken.

"Is everything okay, Mrs. Klein?" Yael asked, and found herself addressing only Margaret's back as she stormed out of the kitchen.

70

Later in the day, I was introducing my date to everyone and finally got to the Kleins, but when my date stuck out her hand to Margaret, saying, "Nice to meet you," Margaret turned on her heel and walked away. Bob Klein gave an embarrassed laugh and took the offered hand. The moment passed, but on my next pass through the kitchen, I asked Yael, "Is there something the matter with Margaret today?"

"The same as every day, just like I told you," Yael answered. And, when I rolled my eyes, she added, "It is because you have a date."

After that day, Margaret's behavior toward me changed. She stopped coming over and was very curt and wouldn't meet my eyes when I met her at the school drop off. Being an old hand at knowing how not to disturb a hive when the queen bee is angry, I started steering clear of her, but I did ask Lauren, who had grown particularly close to Margaret, what was going on.

In the age-old language of the almost teenager, she answered, "Nothing."

With my newly found intuition, I felt a slight chill go through me. Something was going on, but I couldn't for the life of me figure out what it was.

I'd learn about it soon enough but entirely by accident.

A few weeks later, I was passing Lauren's bedroom door, which was slightly ajar, when I heard her talking on the phone. This is what I overheard: "I can't talk anymore just now. My dad just came up the stairs, and he can't hear what we've been talking about, Margaret."

Margaret! What secret conversations could she be having with Margaret?

The next time Margaret called, and I answered the phone, I was ready. I yelled to Lauren to take the call upstairs, and I quietly picked up the downstairs extension and activated a small recording device I had picked up to use during Charlotte's occasional threatening calls. What I heard being said between Lauren and Margaret made the hair on the back of my neck stand up.

Margaret, it seemed, had contacted Charlotte, and the two of them wanted Lauren to somehow get me to admit on audiotape that I had abused her and the other kids. The tape would be corroborating evidence, and then

Margaret would take the stand and would swear to the court she had seen evidence of such abuse. With the recording and Margaret's testimony, Charlotte would get custody of all the children!

"But it's not true," I heard Lauren say during the phone conversation.

"It doesn't matter if it's true or not," Margaret said. "You should lie! Charlotte is your mother, and your father is cruel to keep her children from her. Do you want to be the one who keeps your brothers and sisters away from their own mother? With my testimony, we can make sure the kids go where they belong, and that is with your mom."

I couldn't believe what I was hearing! She was trying to get my daughter to lie to the court system to benefit Charlotte!

I managed to hang the phone up quietly and went to talk this turn of events over with Yael and Shira before deciding what to do.

The nannies didn't seem all that shocked.

"I had a feeling she was up to something," Yael said.

"When she was so angry at the party, I knew she was jealous of your date," agreed Shira.

You could have knocked me over with a feather! It was the first time I had ever been made aware of that subterranean silent conversation that women seem to be able to have with each other that men do not and are seemingly incapable of hearing. Both my nannies had caught all the undercurrents of Margaret's preoccupation with me and my family. I was clueless.

"How do you think Margaret, an older woman, would feel being supplanted in your affections by a younger and prettier woman?" asked Yael.

"In my affections!" I stuttered. "She was just a nice older lady who was good to my kids."

"Not in her mind," said Shira.

"And she is married! What about Bob?" I sputtered.

"What about him?" Yael pointed out dryly. "He pays more attention to the golf tournaments than his wife and kids. He doesn't need her anymore. Women like to be needed."

Wow, the things I didn't know!

So, the nannies and I talked it over, and it was decided I would confront Lauren, who broke down in tears immediately and began apologizing all over the place.

She was a kid, after all, and couldn't be expected to always make the best choices. The adults around her, however, had no such excuse.

I immediately called my lawyer, got a restraining order taken out against Margaret, and had her served with it. I told the kids they were never to go there again, and they never did.

I heard no more from Margaret, except for the new wave of gossip that erupted when Bob divorced her. What is sauce for the goose...

I learned from that sordid situation that not everyone has your best interests at heart, even when they appear to do so. Cynicism isn't something to aim for, but one needn't be a babe in the woods about things either. In my weakened state, I was attracting piranhas.

"I want you to know I will be here for you," Margaret had said and, had I been paying more attention to the ways of the world instead of being so wrapped up in my miserable obsession with my wife, I would have acknowledged that little hint of weirdness my intuition had tried to alert me to and looked that particular gift horse right in the mouth. This was a fine lesson in discernment, learning to take care of myself, and protecting my family.

It gave me more reason than ever to make sure that drawbridge was secure and to work on becoming a strong and resilient man. It was time to man up for real. □

CHAPTER 9
THE MAN IN THE MIRROR

I've been told that the first thing to do when it comes to self-examination is to find out where you stand so you can stand in a better place. I wasn't crazy about the idea of discovering who I was, but my faults and flaws had to be acknowledged if I was serious about changing who I was and manning up. My best thinking had gotten me into the mess in which I found myself, and to correct that thinking, I'd have to make some changes in my life, and that would take a clear perception of myself.

Taking stock of who you are, I assumed, usually occurs around middle age, when you decide if you really are going to buy that red Corvette convertible and have a fling with your administrative assistant. But the time of reckoning had come early for me. I had a lot of self-awareness to catch up on, and to get there, I had to fight through muddy rivers of guilt, chip away at mountains of anger, and cross that most lunar of landscapes—that of looking squarely at myself. I had to learn how to set goals and start achieving them.

I couldn't be a good parent if I was only a shell held together with equal parts determination and desperation. That veneer would crack and there'd be nothing left. I had to stop being a human pinball, bouncing off the flippers and hitting targets by accident. I had to aim my life.

First things first. I started with the "easy" stuff—what was on the outside, like how I looked. All of the stress in my life had exacerbated my hair loss. As with everyone who faces that most visible sign of aging, it didn't make me happy, but with my new resolution to face things as they really were and stop living in a fantasy world, there was no denying that more and more of my scalp was showing every day. So, I bid farewell to the last of my golden blond hair (adios, old friend) and shaved my head. I presented my new bald pate as proudly as Mr. Clean. It felt freeing to not be hiding anymore. Any guy who is losing his hair knows what I mean by hiding. Some grow ponytails to try to divert attention from their rapidly thinning dome. Others try to make the remaining few hairs sort of loop around their head to disguise the fact their bald spot is getting the better of them. Others give the old comb-over a try. All of it, in my opinion, looks as bad as the hair of the man who, when he discovers he is getting gray, dyes it such a dark brown that it looks like a container of shoe polish got dumped on his head.

Leader of the Pack

I had no hair, and now I was going to live with that fact.

Looking into my shaving mirror to examine my new hairless image, I knew that next it was time to head for the full-length mirror and check out what had happened to my body. When I did so, what stared back at me wasn't a guy with "big bones" or "a large frame." This was the boy who had to shop in the "husky" department now grown to manhood. I was legitimately fat and looked like the Michelin Man. My rolls had rolls. I had no muscle definition and couldn't see my toes (much less touch them), and looked like a beached whale—white, clammy, and huge.

It would have been easy for me just to pull down the oversized sweatshirt I was wearing and hide the problem from my own eyes. What wasn't easy was to not just give in to my old friend self-loathing and take to the couch with another bag of chips. Food was, and had always been, comfort for me, but if I were honest, I wasn't feeling comforted by eating anymore. I was just using food to stuff down my feelings for fear they would overwhelm me.

It was time to take on the super-sized me and get healthy. I had a long life ahead of me and lots of people depending on me. I took a deep breath, summoned up my courage and stepped on the bathroom scale. I found I needed to lose 100 pounds!

Did that seem hopeless at first? Absolutely. But my old behavior of giving up wouldn't suit now. I had to look back at what I had gone through so far and had survived, despite my belief I would never make it.

Then I peeked at the future and realized I would need every ounce of physical strength to live through the unknown challenges that awaited me there. It was like there was a giant fallen redwood tree blocking my path and it was up to me to get rid of it. I couldn't move the whole tree at once, but I could make small ax cuts until I had chopped the whole thing into manageable pieces and hauled them out of the path.

I was enjoying wonderful high-calorie meals at home, combined with frequent trips to Pizza Hut or Ming's Garden, and I happily gobbled everything down like a swine. It's as though she had been fattening me up for the kill, and I had been a willing accomplice to my own murder.

Luckily, my father had been a physically strong man, and he had left me that genetic legacy. I called upon it by devising an in-home exercise program, which I stuck to five times a week. Later I would join a gym, but at first, I didn't want anyone to see my shame. (It didn't occur to me that working to get the weight off was the opposite of a shameful activity, and that I should have been proud of my efforts.)

I worked out like a demon, lifting free weights in the garage late at night while the household slept, doing push-ups until my arms burned and sit-ups until my stomach muscles protested so much that to sleep required a handful of ibuprofen. I walked everywhere possible and ran when I could, eventually coming to welcome the time alone and relishing the silence. I threw in exercise whenever I could, a few minutes before work, a half an hour while the kids were doing homework with the nannies, and in the quiet hours when everyone was asleep.

I downed gallons of water, hoping it was true that such a practice would flush out fat, and gave up soda. I also put down all snacks and desserts, and quelled any mutinous hunger with carrot sticks and almonds. I became best friends with the salad bar whenever we went out to eat, and stuck to protein and vegetables at home. The kids at first made fun of me, but sooner than even I thought, results started showing and the mocking stopped. Yael and Shira were delighted, as they had, they later confessed, been worried about my health. They knew they wouldn't always be with the kids but wanted to make sure someone would, and I was their chosen candidate.

Losing weight was great for my self-esteem. It was a visible sign that positive changes were being made in my life. And those external changes weren't the only ones happening. I knew that I had to learn to treat myself better in other ways, and one of those ways was by giving myself permission to start having more fun.

I had something in mind, but first I had to battle past the obstacles that my own mind put in my way:

You don't have time.

The kids need you.

You shouldn't be spending money on yourself like this.

You could get hurt.

It's dangerous.

See, what I wanted to do was to make a childhood dream of mine come true. I wanted to learn to drive a race car!

After many mental arguments, I joined the BMW club and signed up for beginner's driving classes. Putting on that helmet and climbing into the car was one of the highest highs I've ever had. I was strapped into the passenger's seat in the cockpit and, once the engine was fired up, the instructor asked me, "Are you ready?" and I gave him the thumbs-up. Off we went, flying around the track, and I have never felt so exhilarated. Watching the signs on the wall fly past and the people in the infield turning into blurs, I had never felt so free.

I was hooked right away and couldn't wait to go again. The day I was finally allowed to drive the car myself felt like heaven to me. All my troubles took a backseat, and the immediacy of the next lap marker, the curve coming up, and the digits on the speedometer were all that mattered. I was living in the moment, and the dread and fear and worry blew away like the dust from the tires.

Maybe it was the moments racing, when my brain was momentarily freed from my fears, troubles, and obsessions that gave me enough of a pause to allow other thoughts to finally start to come into my consciousness. Maybe it was just the passage of time or the fact that we, as humans, can take only so much despair before we either break or change, but whatever it was, I knew the time had come for me to tackle the toughest part of my self-reclamation—the inner man.

I didn't go to a shrink (I'd had enough of therapy when I had been court-ordered to attend sessions with my kids), didn't get religion (although I now know a higher power was straightening out my thinking), didn't vent to a close friend, didn't pray (at least in the way I thought of prayer); I just responded to a deep feeling that I had to change. It was as though I had been looking at my life through murky glass, which suddenly cleared like a foggy mirror after a shower.

I started to look back at my marriage and, without the blinders of obsession, began to see what I had felt for Charlotte wasn't even real love. At first, it was desperate gratitude that someone as beautiful as she was would even deign to look at someone as lowly as me. Then it turned into an exercise in self-flagellation. She beat me up emotionally, and I not only let her, I stood in the ring with my hands down in devotion to take whatever punishment she handed out. Of course, the more pain I took, the more she gave.

Not only did she hold me in contempt, but I had held myself in contempt. I became a perpetual supplicant, laying treasures at the foot of the queen hoping she would show me favor. I became a virtual slave, working constantly, running ever faster on a hamster wheel of my own making trying to please her. There was no shared partnership, no returned affection. The whole relationship between us was toxic from the beginning and only got fouler as time went on. That wasn't love—that was an addiction, and I was an addict, and my drug of choice was Charlotte.

I was as sick as they come, but I could feel the chains on my spirit beginning to loosen.

The shackle that first gave way was the one holding in the anger. When my spirit started to rebound, what I found bubbling up in me was an absolute rage at what Charlotte had done—not even so much to me, but to our children. I applied what I was discovering about stuffing feelings down (and the delayed harm that caused) and let myself feel the feeling. I literally boiled with anger, but took it out on the speed bag in the garage, punching as hard and fast as I could until the leather frayed. Finally, the day came when I discovered that the anger had lifted. I could let it go.

I saw Charlotte for what she was as opposed to what I had wanted her to be all those years. She was selfish, manipulative, and self-involved, and I and my kids were better off without her.

My feelings were confirmed later when I got a call from her brother—who had begun acting as a go-between whenever Charlotte wanted something from me.

Charlotte was willing to settle and accept one large payment immediately in lieu of the rest of the lifetime alimony she was owed. It turns out that during the time of our divorce proceedings, when she had been living with the cop in Manhattan, he and she had produced two children (despite the fact that she was still married to me). Once she had those kids, their relationship predictably had begun to unravel. Charlotte was always super secretive, and her stories changed like the weather, but I heard through the grapevine that she had accused the cop of abuse, bolted from their house (leaving him stranded with the two kids and unpaid bills for thousands of dollars), and headed for the police department to offer to testify against him and several other cops about possible corruption if she were granted immunity and entered a witness protection program. She was accepted into the program, had her name legally changed and got a new Social Security number (which came in handy to help keep those debtors from finding her), and would be hitting the road, my money in hand, to ride off into the sunset to pick her next victim.

I paid the almost quarter-million-dollar lump sum, realizing as I did so, I was being given two gifts: one, clarity to see who she really had been all along—a grifter, a con artist, a snake-oil salesperson who had pegged me (correctly) for her mark—and two, a get-out-of-jail card for our marriage. I wrote the check as soon as I could get to a pen and, with that payment, neither I, nor my children, ever heard a word from her again. I consider that payoff cheap at any price—even if I had to borrow to the hilt to do it, and even though my children and I had to do without some things.

Though by my nature I felt bad about what my children had been put through, and was all too ready to take it all on my own shoulders, I tried my best to steer my thinking into new pathways. I worked hard on not just accepting my first thought about the situation but untangling the threads one by one, trying to find some I might have overlooked before. Was there a new way to view various incidents that had happened to me?

As I got better at looking back over the past without that fogged vision, I could see more clearly that, though I had acted and reacted badly much of the time, Charlotte had acted worse.

Little by little, I shook off the mantle of guilt I had carried with me since the minute Charlotte had even expressed she was unhappy. I finally arrived at the crystal-clear thought that I was responsible for exactly 50 percent of the train wreck that was my marriage.

With that revelation, I could start to acknowledge that, though I had been blind sometimes and misguided often, I didn't know what I didn't know and had done nothing out of malice. I really had been doing the best I knew how to do at the time and, though I felt stinging humiliation and shame looking back at some of my behavior, I had meant her and our children no harm.

After sitting with those thoughts for a while, it came to me that I was forgiving myself, which made it easier to forgive Charlotte. By forgiving her, I would be doing myself a great favor. She would no longer be able to control my life, whether through misplaced love or pathetic eagerness to please, or through the recent bitterness and anger I had felt toward her. I would live without those corrosive emotions that had tied me to her, and I knew that would make me not only freer but a better father and a better man.

I then practiced doing something that seemed entirely foreign to me. I searched for things for which I deserved a pat on the back. What had I done right in this mess?

I tried to get past the low-hanging fruit, like the fact that I was a good wage earner and a hard worker, and went a little deeper. I finally came to the realization that I deserved some credit for not cutting and running when things had hit the fan. I had stayed for my children and put one foot in front of the other every day even though I sometimes wanted only to die.

I had learned to ask for help and accept that help when given. I had overcome soul-crushing depression, forced myself out of an emotional fetal position, and stopped whining long enough to start to stand on my own two feet. I tried to keep my heart open enough to exchange love with my kids. I had started trusting my own instincts and begun to make decisions for myself and my children that would help steer a course out of the storm and into calmer waters. I had taken charge of my body and was striving to be healthier, both physically and mentally. It took some time, but I had begun, inch by painful inch, to pull myself up by my bootstraps, and my family with me.

I wasn't perfect, but I was doing my best, and that wasn't nothing. I was learning to man up.☐

CHAPTER 10
EXCUSE ME, I'VE GOT A LIFE TO RUN HERE

It was repeatedly pointed out to me, by some truly helpful friends, that my kids could not be my "all." I had a business to run and a social life to construct, and (gasp!) I might even have wanted to consider having sex again in this lifetime.

I was not ready to hear any of that for a very long time. But, like a rock with water dripping on it, my resistance finally eroded and I made my first tentative forays into life beyond the disaster.

***

What I didn't know about women would fill a book (or a library), but once I was able to take an actual full breath without the world coming down around my ears, I did acknowledge that I was craving adult companionship from members of the opposite sex. While this might be construed as "horniness" by some of you (and true to a point), I actually was lonely.

The kids were developing their own lives and interests (a fact I was very glad of, as it was concrete proof that they were slowly moving past the trauma they had endured), and the nannies had returned to Israel. Yael and Shira had helped pull us out of hell, and we were all sorry to see them go, but they both would always be family to us and we to them.

As they were packing to leave, Yael had pulled me aside, taken both of my hands in hers, and looked deeply in my eyes.

"You are going to be fine, Mr. Matt," she said. "You know what to do now, and I know you can do it. You are a good man, and I have faith in you."

Yael's faith in me meant a lot. Having someone be proud of me and believe I was capable of doing the right thing still felt a little strange, but was much appreciated.

I wasn't totally free of poor self-esteem, of course. Echoes of self-criticism still bounced off the canyons of my mind, and I still occasionally second-guessed my decisions, but more and more I trusted my own instincts and things managed to turn out fairly well. Those times gave me confidence and, as we got further away from the edge of the pit of horror that was Charlotte, the more courage I had.

Waving goodbye to the plane taking Yael and Shira off to Israel, I felt a quick clench of icy fingers of fear around my heart, but I felt as ready as I would ever be to steer my family down the road—no matter how bumpy or twisted that road might be.

One thing I vowed was, no more total strangers in our lives. Everyone had to be referred to me to get past the velvet rope. It was as though they needed a passport and a visa and extreme vetting to get in. No nannies, au pairs, well-meaning friends, creepy neighbors, or anyone other than us. My family was becoming an isolationist nation. I would pull in our borders, defend what was ours, and make forays outside the wall only very carefully.

At least I thought I was being careful...

I broke one cardinal rule of dating right away—I fell for a co-worker. It seems inevitable in hindsight. I was a walking vulnerability, the very definition of a man ready for a rebound relationship, even though what I was rebounding from was a nightmare.

I was instantly attracted to Jessica. She was pretty, soft-spoken, quick to smile, and always ready to laugh, even though she had troubles of her own. It seemed she had a somewhat uncaring boyfriend, and their relationship was hitting the skids. With increasing frequency (because I am nothing if not possessed of a sympathetic ear), she started telling me about her relationship and talking over the arguments and problems as they popped up. I shared a little about what I had gone through, and we compared notes. Talking about it seemed to help Jessica shed some of her burden, and for my part, I would have listened to her forever, just to keep her face turned toward mine.

Eventually we found ourselves sharing a ride home, parked outside a diner in a storm, and talking as we always did. But the conversation was interrupted when I found her in my arms. I don't know if I reached for her or she reached for me, but I didn't care. We were suddenly wildly kissing, and I felt I might die of happiness. I had never kissed a woman other than Charlotte in my life. Matt the late bloomer was making up for lost time.

Jessica's boyfriend got the ax after that, and she and I began seeing each other as often as possible. It was she who made her appearance at that fated barbecue where Margaret transformed from helpful neighbor into vindictive villain.

I was unaware about the Margaret situation unfolding, and I was just as clueless about Jessica's introduction to my family. I thought I was fooling my kids by being all casual about introducing them to Jessica amidst the crowd at the party. But I wasn't getting away with it. The minute Jessica left, my kids pounced en masse like a pride of lions feeding on a wildebeest.

"Is she your new girlfriend, Dad?" said Lauren.

"Are you getting married again?" asked Emily with a flicker of fear in her eyes.

"Is she moving into our house, Dad?" Ethan, who always cut to the chase, chimed in.

Abigail, always the ray of sunshine, added, "I think she's pretty," and Aaron said nothing, of course, but he stayed to listen intently to my answers.

"No, no, it's nothing like that. She's just a friend," I protested.

They didn't believe a word of it, and that's because it wasn't true. (Another lesson of parenting: always be real with your kids. They will see right through you if you are not.) I wanted my relationship with Jessica to be much more than a friendship. I was in love.

Jessica and I stayed together for nearly a year, and during that time she did much to help me build myself up and repair my heart. The sex was restorative, of course. It was like learning a new language—making love to a woman who enjoyed it and wasn't just using me as a procreation machine, and who liked me for who I was. The entire experience was as relaxing and comfortable as taking a long vacation.

Also, once I got past the clanging clamor that was the need for sex, I learned how to actually communicate normally with a woman. I was scared at first of offering differing opinions (after what I'd gone through, I was sure I would have my head torn off for disagreeing), but Jessica was centered enough in herself not only to allow differing opinions but welcome them. What do you know? She actually had room to let both of us be individuals in our relationship. That was a revelation—as was having an argument without her threatening suicide or murder. Jessica stood her ground and never threatened to leave, and that let me learn how to stand my ground and defend my position or else listen to her side and decide (not feel compelled) to agree with her. She didn't bellow or threaten or sob. Her equilibrium helped me to find my own. Having been faced only with extreme drama prior to this, I didn't know how to do anything except shut up and shut down. My time with Jessica changed this.

We had a very nice time together with lots of laughter and many tender moments. I hope I was as good an agent for healing her heart as she was for mine. But, in the end, a decision had to be made.

I wanted her to be with me forever. She didn't prevaricate or stall or lie her way out of the answer to spare my feelings, but gave me the respect of being honest with me. She was not ready to be a stepmother to five kids. That was perfectly reasonable and not to be argued with, so we parted company.

But where to next? I didn't see myself as a man who was going to go through life without a woman.

Once my friends knew this, of course, they kept setting me up on blind dates, saying, "I've got someone you have to meet…"

Though I am sure those words have begun more than one successful relationship, I'm even surer that they have cracked open the door to more mansions of horror than a Vincent Price movie. I would eventually meet someone through these helpful buddies, but first I had to live through one of the most devious institutions ever devised by mankind: online dating.

Oy, as my parents would have said. Online dating is slightly rough even on those beautiful people—the confident, tall, handsome men with perfectly white teeth and women who look like Heidi Klum—but to the rest of us nebbishes, the experience is brutal.

There must be something about the anonymity of the internet that brings out the worst in people. As if it weren't enough to have to endure the process of having to dissect oneself in a questionnaire that sounds like a sadistic psychologist devised it, one also has to post photos and waken every dragon of self-doubt that has ever lurked in one's consciousness. "I look fat. Oh no, my head is shining in this one. Should I be smiling? Will she think I look like a used-car salesman? But this one where I am frowning makes me look like a serial killer. Do I post a photo of me and the kids? All the kids? She will run screaming into the night before I get a chance to meet her. Maybe I could Photoshop a few of the kids out…"

What a mental dialogue that whole process began! And all to impress a sight-unseen perfect stranger, who might herself look like a Green Bay Packers defensive lineman on a bad day but is posting photos that show only her surprisingly attractive left eyebrow.

I felt like a fraud and a fool, but I did it anyway. Such is the hunt for romance in our times.

I did have a firm grip on one principle I was not willing to surrender, however.

I was not willing to be abused or otherwise treated badly in any way by anyone for any reason anymore. No relationship was worth that, and I knew that from hard experience. I also knew no one could love me if I didn't love myself, so I stopped all those mental self-criticisms the online dating process seemed to be designed to set in motion, and I ventured forth as bravely and honestly as I could.

I got some "nibbles" right away. Some were just wrong for me from the outset. (Why do married women solicit on dating sites? What would I do with a 19-year-old Ukrainian? Yes, I did mind that she used to be a man.) Others just took advantage of the facelessness of the sites to tell me what an ugly, stupid, or undesirable guy I was. (Keep your opinions to yourself, trolls.) Others commented that the thought of five kids scared them off (I understood that one). But some seemed okay to me, and I went on several dates—mostly first dates. These seemed to me to be slightly awkward job interviews and were rarely any fun. Certainly, none produced any spark, and one was highly memorable only because it showed that my resolve not to be treated badly was a sound one.

Marina responded to my post almost immediately and asked if we could talk. I checked out her profile, and she seemed to be a good candidate—the right age, a working professional, not bad-looking, educated, and seemingly intelligent. I asked if we could meet somewhere for coffee. She messaged me right back, telling me to call her right away. When I did, she told me where to meet her for dinner the next night, a pricey steakhouse in Manhattan. "A take-charge woman," I thought. Nothing new to me.

I showed up at the appointed time—shaved, showered, and looking my best—and, after giving my name to the maître d', took a seat at a small table and waited for Marina. Almost 20 minutes later, in walked a disheveled, unkempt, poorly dressed woman in shambles who bore only a passing resemblance to her photo online.

"I'm Marina," she said to me, not even offering her hand, and to a passing waiter, "I'll have a double martini."

I don't drink, so this took me aback a little, but that was only the beginning. Marina proceeded to order the most expensive steak on the menu and to talk, nonstop, through the whole meal. She went on and on about her unhappy online experiences. "The men were all boring sh—s," she said, "with nothing to offer a woman like me" and "most of them were only after sex anyway." (I understood the drive of lust in the male of the species, but looking at and listening to her, I thought she might defeat a bottle of Viagra.) None of them had any money or good jobs or understood she was in a 12-step program (which one was not specified, but after her second double martini, I was betting it wasn't AA), and some of them were even married!

When she wound down long enough for me to get a word in edgewise, I told her a little about myself—that I had been married but was now divorced, and was raising five children. Marina put down her fork long enough to comment.

"You talk too much," she said, and I thought she was kidding, but she wasn't.

She took up where she left off, except this time she peppered me with questions.

"What do you do for a living?" "Where do you live?" "Did you rent or own your house?" I felt like I was applying for a mortgage.

Something I said (and I think it was the fact that I owned a successful business) must have passed her muster, because she suddenly got up, told me to order her the crème brûlée and that she had to go to the "little girl's room" (that appellation right there would have been enough for me to never have a second date with someone). Off she went. The dessert arrived. Marina had been gone so long, I thought she had slipped out a back door. I used the time to mentally review some of my new, but firmly held, convictions.

I would no longer suffer at the hands of an abuser. Marina was an abuser. She was rude, controlling, and self-centered. I deserved better than that. I deserved a kind, mannerly, educated woman with a nice temperament, a calm demeanor and a good sense of humor, who liked me for who I was and not what I could give her. My time with Marina helped bring that into sharp focus. To make sure I got the point, the lesson was driven home to me in the starkest manner.

After 20 minutes, when I realized she had left and stuck me with the not-insubstantial check, Marina returned...at least I thought it was Marina. I had to look carefully. Her hair was styled and gleaming, held back with jeweled clips. She had changed the rags she had worn for a form-fitting cashmere sweater and pencil skirt, and exchanged her muck boots for black stilettos. She had done a complete makeup job—from lipstick and blush to several shades of eye shadow and even false eyelashes! She had on a tasteful gold necklace, several bangle bracelets, and lovely hoop earrings. As she passed by my chair to sit, I even noted that she smelled good! It was one of the strangest things I'd ever seen anyone do (other than things my ex-wife did, of course. She was the queen of strange).

I briefly entertained the idea of standing up and just walking out (as abusers deserved from those they attempted to abuse), but instead decided I would make use of the situation as a practice session. I would test out the muscles I had never used before—my charm muscles—to see if I change the power ratio in this relationship. She thought she was running the show. I wanted to see if I could run it instead.

I stood up when she returned to the table, a mannerly trick I had learned from old Cary Grant movies and sat when she sat, smiling my brightest smile. I told her, in a slightly husky voice, that I had missed her. I purposefully directed the force of my personality at her like a tractor beam, and what do you know?

She was totally and thoroughly charmed.

It seems Marina saved up her ammo for men she considered good catches, and I had made the grade. Lucky me. She resumed talking a mile a minute as though she had never been interrupted. She would love to see my place of business. Did I have a corner office? She would bet I paid myself quite a salary. She herself was an executive (I didn't dare interrupt to ask her, "An executive what?"). She wasn't paid enough for her efforts, though, and one really did need two salaries to live the right kind of life, didn't I agree? Did I like to travel? She loved to travel, and perhaps we could take a trip together. (She had, it appeared, conveniently forgotten I had five kids, or maybe she thought they were all in boarding school or all confined to their nursery with Mary Poppins.)

While she rattled on, I mentally turned down the sound and watched her facial expressions. She really was batting her eyelashes (or whoever's eyelashes she was wearing) at me! It was like watching the Muppets with the volume off. She kept reaching over to touch my hand as she spoke, and when she grabbed both my hands, I tuned back in to the conversation.

"Would you like to come to my place?" she said in a seductive whisper.

"Not tonight, dear," I said, knowing full well that wild horses couldn't have dragged me anywhere near Marina again. I paid the tab to get the hell out of there, allowed her a quick kiss on the cheek as I put her in a cab, and ignored the many texts and emails I got over the next week. Marina had been a good object lesson for me. Remember, Matt: no relationship is worth taking abuse over. I was worth more than that. I didn't have to be the one feeling lonely and ill-treated. I could be charming, gregarious, and attractive, sexy even. I had a lot to offer the right woman.

I would soon find out I had a lot to offer the wrong woman too.

I refined my search criteria after Marina, and my definition of the perfect woman for me took a slight left turn. I didn't need just a sex partner or a woman in whom I had a romantic interest. I was attracting the wrong type of relationship hunting for those things. Instead, I went back to searching for someone to fill what I had always thought was the most virtuous of women's roles. I began looking for someone who could help mother my kids.

What a recipe for disaster.☐

CHAPTER 11
ONCE MORE UNTO THE BREACH

Though I had been a great one for dragging my kids (sometimes court-ordered, sometimes not) to psychologists, sociologists, counselors, and therapists, I never went to one for myself.

No doubt, somewhere in me I thought two things, both equally untrue: the kids were the important ones. They needed the help. And, buried deeper: I don't have a problem. Look how I well I was handling this dire situation. I deserved a medal, not a shrink.

A woman I knew was a brilliant pediatric surgeon and mother to a little girl. I hadn't seen her in a while when I ran into her while making a run for coffee in town. The usual "How have you been?" question unlocked a spigot in her, and she let loose with a tale of woe. It seems her husband had left her, and they had joint custody of their daughter. Even though she had plenty of money and a live-in nanny, caring for her one child had been too much for her. It had gotten so bad that her parents had to move into her house to parent the little girl while my friend, the mother, was committed to an inpatient mental hospital, having had a "nervous collapse."

"If that's what happened to me trying to care for one kid, I can't even imagine what you are going through caring for five," she said. "You are an inspiration."

Yup, that's me—just give me a cape and I am a regular superhero.

Except I had no cape or, for that matter, any superpowers, and without a therapist (or a clue) and relying only on my own best judgment, I took my eye off the ball and put my foot in it up to the thighbone...again.

I met Marnie on a blind date set up by a friend and, at first glance, she seemed a great match.

She was a drop-dead gorgeous French-born red head, with deep blue eyes, was highly-educated, and best of all in my distorted view, a mother herself. She had been married and gained custody of her only child, a son, so surely, she would make a good mother to my brood too, right? I clung to the notion that women were instinctively better parents long after the evidence seen by my own eyes should have disproved that idea. But they aren't kidding when they say, "Denial is not a river in Egypt."

Marnie was a medical doctor working in New York. She didn't make much money, as she had come to the profession late, but she had an impressive occupation and that sounded good to me. She was 33, so therefore close enough to me in age too. She appeared perfect.

We dated for two years. During that time, she was good with my kids, all of whom liked her, with the glaring exception of Lauren. The two of them apparently hated each other on sight, but I chalked that up to jealously on Lauren's part, not prescience. I was swayed in my opinion because Marnie was very nice to me—at least at the beginning of our relationship. She also seemed like a caring and competent mother to her son, Henry.

If Marnie had any flaw in my eyes, it was that she was a little overly emotional at times—a bit up and down, I would say. But considering that I have five kids, and considering how bad Charlotte was in that way, handling Marnie's moods seemed like a walk in the park—and something I should do for a woman willing to be with all of us. Marnie also seemed to be smarter with money. She was very adamant about my bringing more money home from my business and putting it in the bank—"for a rainy day," she would say. We had somehow survived Charlotte's years of bleeding us dry and now, with my business doing a bit better, we were on a slight upward trajectory. I didn't know if I would ever lose my fear of financial insecurity, but I didn't want to appear like a tightwad to Marnie, so I gave her money to put away and buy pretty much whatever she wanted—I felt obligated to her for helping me with my five kids. That felt like love to me.

Marnie and her son moved in with us, and while I never felt like Henry was one of my own, he was a nice enough kid and no problem. Marnie (aided by a live-in and very hard-working housekeeper/nanny) did help with my own children (despite the ongoing fight between her and Lauren). That helpful relationship she had with the rest of my kids was the basis for the slightly startling statement Marnie made to me as we approached our second year together.

"I have been good to you and your kids, haven't I, Matt?" When I agreed that was true, she went on. "I disrupted my life and the life of my son to move in with you and help with your children," she said. "So, we need to get married now."

Put that way with clear black-and-white logic (and with the remnants of my behavior of obeying women's commands kicking in,) I couldn't see any objection to her proposal. No warning bells or distant clanging alarms went off in my head. Or perhaps I just didn't hear them. Perhaps I didn't want to hear them. I wanted a partner and my family to be safe and complete around me. I wanted the loneliness to end.

Marnie and I were married at the town hall two weeks later on September 18, 2001, (we had wanted to do it on September 11, 2001, but the judge was on vacation), with only the cops who happened to be there at the time as witnesses. Little did I know I could have used them in a professional capacity, as a crime was being committed right under our noses. Another con was being perpetrated, and another viper had just sunk its teeth into my neck.

Marnie hadn't wanted my children present at the ceremony. "Let's make it just the two of us," she said, and I saw that as a romantic gesture, rather than what it was: divide and conquer. Maybe Lauren had caught on to Marnie's true intentions. Maybe she had even confronted Marnie about being a gold digger. Maybe Marnie was worried that Lauren would cause a scene and try to stop the ceremony. I don't know. I wasn't paying attention. I was in love.

From the moment the ink was dry on the wedding certificate, Marnie's behavior toward me started to change, and it got worse the whole time we were together. By the end of our marriage, it was total hell…again.

The first big change was that Marnie moved her mother and adult brother into our home. They were immigrants without a place to live, and we couldn't turn them away, could we?

Oddly, they required only one room since they wanted to share. (I thought that was a little strange, but hey, doesn't every family have their own oddball characteristics?) Marnie argued that their presence meant there were more hands on deck to help with the kids. It was quite a crowd, I had to agree. Since her mother and brother wouldn't be working except by helping with my kids, they'd need some money for their services. They went on the payroll. Also, the house was too busy for any of them to manage, which is why I also said it was fine that we hire a housekeeper, a Filipino woman named Betty. She went on the payroll. I was suddenly bankrolling a cast of thousands. That fear of financial insecurity reared his head again, but I pushed it back down under the surface. We'd be fine. I'd just have to work a little harder and longer hours to make ends meet. Maybe Marnie would be able to help a little. She was a doctor, after all.

Yes, I was the guy who would buy the Brooklyn Bridge from you.

I so wanted a partner, a fellow parent, someone to care for my kids (and me), someone with whom to share life's ups and downs, that I didn't see that the movement happening around us wasn't just the growing pains of the members of a blended family adjusting to one another, but the first rumblings of an earthquake headed our way.

Marnie quit working right away, so I was the sole supporter of my now expanded family.

Marnie spent her days doing three things: hiding money, drinking, and listening to her mother and brother nag and pick at her. I wasn't sure what the problem was, as her mother rattled off things to Marnie in French, a language I don't speak, but whatever they were arguing about, Marnie took it hard and her drinking picked up speed. First it was a bit too much wine at night, then she began drinking during the day, then it became a 24-hour marathon event. I was pretty surprised by this turn of events, but other than mentioning the increase, which caused Marnie to erupt in a torrent of anger, I couldn't think of what to do about it.

The ground under our feet started falling away even faster when one of my kids, detaching from her siblings, all of whom were trying to be brave and supportive of my decision, confessed that their new stepmother, uncle, and grandmother were mistreating them the minute I left the house every day.

They were being screamed at, denied privileges, even food, and threatened by violence. The girls were told they were fat and stupid and no one would ever love them. The boys were yelled at, humiliated, and abused.

My wife became a daily drunk, and as her drinking increased, so did the level of shrieking insanity in the house. My wife began emotional manipulation worthy of Guantanamo. One child would be singled out by her, and the others made to ostracize that child or face their stepmother's wrath themselves. The chosen child (often Abigail at age 12) would be insulted and mocked, given slop to eat, and be made to feel like he or she didn't deserve to live. It was sibling against sibling, and my family started to crack apart.

I should have noticed, of course. The boys' grades were falling, and I was getting called by teachers and principals about their behavior. Emily's tears had begun again, but this time, intimidated as she was, they fell behind closed doors. Aaron talked less and less as though he were trying to disappear entirely. My wife complained to me that the kids were disrespectful and unruly, yet she taught them I was the unstable one, ready to explode in uncontrollable rages. She made sure my kids couldn't even turn to me for comfort.

Lauren told me later she could not wait to graduate high school and get out of that house, as everyone—even me—had turned against her on Marnie's instructions. (Aaron, Lauren confided, had risked his stepmother's wrath and gave Lauren surreptitious hugs on the sly, whispering, "I love you.") Though I can see how Lauren felt that I had turned on her too, the truth was that I had only pretended to go along with the ostracism. When I didn't, Marnie's fury doubled and the "offending" kid got treated much worse. It was like being prisoners in our own home again.

When my wife's brother, a giant of a man, raised his fist to my 14-year-old daughter one night, I felt something in me shift. It took her courageous revelation of that terrifying encounter to open my eyes. Wanting only to share the responsibility for the children's upbringing, I had instead shirked my responsibility.

I felt burning shame.

Marnie grew more hostile toward me and the kids—even her own kid—so there was constant turmoil in the house. It began to feel very familiar around there.

The sense of déjà vu reached its pinnacle when, one Friday night as we were lighting the traditional Sabbath candles before dinner, Marnie came to the table obviously drunk, slurring her words and weaving visibly. Ethan let loose a quick laugh at the sight and I, by instinct, reached up to grab the wineglass Marnie threw just before it hit Ethan's skull. What flashed in my mind was that night in the kitchen with blood running down Ethan's face when he had been struck by the coffee cup his mother had flung at him. I saw the scene clearly in my mind's eye. I said to myself, Oh, my God, I've done it again.

I had exposed my children to danger and trauma and again put myself in a situation where I was a victim. I realized then what that expression meant, "There are no victims, only volunteers." I had stepped right up and signed up for this situation again after suffering through the horror of it once before. How could I have not seen or even gotten an inkling of what had been headed our way?

I had to find a way out of this for me and my kids that wouldn't kill us all—maybe even literally. I think right then and there, I sent a subconscious plea to some unknown higher power asking for help and the strength to get through whatever lay ahead for us.

Marnie's mother and brother had joined in the hostile behavior aimed at the children and me. Someone was always being grounded or punished, or was in their room in tears when I came home. Henry finally couldn't take it and ran away. Lauren got out as often as she could, staying out with friends rather than facing the chaos at home. She left home the second she graduated from high school. But the rest of us seemed trapped.

Constantly, at Marnie's side like a pair of vampire bats, her mother and brother were hissing in her ear, fast and furious in frantic whispers. I couldn't understand what they said but came to believe, because of the sidelong glances and gestures, that the conversations were about me. As I was to learn, I was right in the assumption. Marnie's family wanted her to divorce me and take me for everything I was worth. It had been their plan from the beginning.

With the added pressure of her family in her ear, Marnie started adding pills to the daily mix of alcohol she consumed, and her behavior grew even more erratic.

One night, when Lauren was home from college visiting, I left our master bedroom to go say goodnight to the girls. When I returned to bed, Marnie looked like a woman possessed. Her hair was a wild tangle, her eyes were red-rimmed, and her hands, like claws, were aimed at my face.

"You f—king liar," she shrieked. "You said you went to say goodnight to Emily and Abigail, not Lauren! I heard you. You were talking to that bitch Lauren! How dare you? I'm going to kill you," and she launched off the bed. She wheeled on me and screamed, "I hate you and I want you dead, you lying piece of sh—," and she left, slamming the bedroom door. I had no idea what she was ranting about, only that she was mentally unstable and dangerous and might actually want me dead. I let her go and didn't follow her.

Marnie moved into the room vacated by her son, with her mother and brother—she lived there for a year. She and her family cut the children off and stopped speaking to us all (a mercy under the circumstances). It was as though a line had been taped on the floor, separating the two sides of the family and the house. These artificial demilitarized zones went on for a year.

One night, Marnie came to my room dressed quite provocatively and said in a sexy voice, "Oh, Matt, it has gone so wrong between us. Can't we turn this around?" She gave me a smoldering look. I knew I was being set up for something, and I couldn't let that happen.

I wasn't buying what she was selling, and I said, "Marnie, I have tolerated how you and your family spoke and acted toward me and the kids for too long, and I won't stand it anymore."

"But Matt..." she began.

"If you can name me one thing you have done wrong in this marriage, I'd be willing to speak to you about a reconciliation," I said, knowing she couldn't do such a thing.

Her demeanor changed immediately.

"I haven't done anything wrong. I'm the victim here. It's you who are always denying me what I want. A reconciliation! I don't want to stay with you a second longer than I have to. I never did, you stupid little man. You disgust me. My mother wanted me to divorce you years ago, but I stuck around hoping you'd give me all the money I'm entitled to. You treat me and my family like sh——. Everything is about your precious brats, and I hate every one of them and you, too. Go f—k yourself." And she marched out the door.

Finally, I had had enough. I felt the last shred of feeling I had for Marnie withered in me like a vine in the winter wind. But I had desperately wanted to avoid another divorce. I wasn't sure that I had the physical strength to live through the experience again and wanted to spare my family the convulsion, but I knew then it had to be done.

I waited to have her serve me papers, and then I made her a ridiculously generous settlement offer so she and her family would just go away (it was then that I found out they had been draining my bank accounts for years). She rejected the offer so, even though it would be hard to sustain and would jeopardize my business, I offered her 90 percent of my assets. Again, she rejected the offer. She wanted 110 percent.

While this legal wrangling was going on, Marnie's attorney made a motion to optimize support in family court. Instead of the $3,500 a month I was offering her (remember, she had no child to support, as her son was an adult and I had already paid for his college), she wanted $8,000 a month!

How was I supposed to get that kind of money? I was still paying Charlotte almost that much per month in equitable distribution with many years left on the 20-year payout.

Sell the 8-bedroom house I had built her ("A palace for my princess," I had named the house when she asked me to build it for her), borrow money from the business, and get a loan from everyone I knew— that was the answer from her attorney. Marnie knew how Charlotte had raked me over the financial coals and didn't see why she deserved any less.

Marnie even wanted me to throw into the settlement the Mont Blanc pen she had gotten me as a gift, and she demanded to keep my mother's ring and her own son's watch! She had already stripped the house of everything of value, right down to the clock on the wall and the family silver. She literally would have taken the clothes off our backs if she could have figured out a way to resell them.

I was ready to let it all go just to get free of her and her poisonous family.

Marnie's family even took my mother's emerald ring and a Rolex watch I had given Henry for his graduation that he had inadvertently left behind. It was easy to see they were packing to leave. I was hoping they would go with no violence. I knew if the brother raised his hand again to any of my kids, I would be the one getting violent.

I had been warned that there was a class action suit against the judge in front of whom we were to appear, due to her blatant discrimination against men in divorce cases, so I was braced for the worst. With my luck in family court, I wouldn't have been surprised if I were stripped of everything I owned and hauled off in shackles just for breathing. But, for once in my life, I was pleasantly surprised at the judge's findings. She told Marnie there was no reason to grant her motion that her support payment double, because Marnie, as an experienced physician, should be working within three months. "Go get a job," is basically what the judge said. We settled the case a few weeks later. Marnie got almost a million dollars (paid with the money my mom had left me when she passed away a few years earlier).

I was free once more.

I never spoke to Marnie again, but her son later contacted me for a job reference and told me the rest of the story. Marnie, it seemed, had tried to practice medicine again, but because of her continued drinking and use of drugs, she had failed. The mother had died, and the brother, who was still sharing his mother's room at the time, killed himself soon afterward. There was no further word from Marnie, and her son got no answer at her last known New York address.

That's all I know, and it's more than I needed to know. I was not curious about Marnie's fate—only relieved, beyond belief, at mine.

Finally, and for the first time in 20 years, my family and I were truly living in peace. No one was screaming or yelling or calling anyone a filthy name. No one was draining my bank account. The tears stopped again. Laughter returned. I cleaned and fixed up the house and sold it. That place had nothing but bad memories for us, and the time for bad memories was behind us...at last.□

CHAPTER 12
TAKING RIGHT ACTION

The way to build self-esteem is to do estimable acts or, as the Torah puts it, the way to gain courage is to act bravely. It was time to do the right thing.

After I got rid of my second wife and her family, I felt mighty relieved at first, and I know that my children did too. The tension in our house went from our being able to cut it with a knife to being a low buzz that would remain with us for a long time as we all healed in our own ways.

For myself, I had a lot of thinking to do. How had I let such a terrible thing happen...again? How had I walked right into the bear trap and not seen that I had all but fastened the sharp metal teeth around my own ankle? What delusional thinking did I allow to flourish to make myself believe that my children needed the love of a woman—any woman—as a stand-in for a mother figure? With our track record in the maternal department, they were obviously much better off with just me.

"Just me" was the phrase with which I had to begin my soul-searching. Again my actions had declared I didn't believe I was enough, that I was "less than," not up to the job of raising my kids or even walking through life under my own power. The kids needed a mother; I needed a partner— both those conclusions were false and, in our case, destructive.

It was time to put such thinking in the past and realize that I was being given all I needed to be both a good parent and a good man. "Being given" was my nod to my murky notion that maybe—just maybe—there was a Something looking out for me and my children. I gave the Something no face and didn't reference Him in my daily life—not even calling out for help when I surely needed it. But there was Something or Someone right at the periphery of my vision and, every now and then, I gave It a perfunctory nod.

I went to work every day (I had to build my business up again after it took a financial hit from the crash in my industry and my settlement with Marnie) and went through all the motions of my daily life, but the whole time I was also having this internal dialogue with myself. I was taking an inventory of what I had done or not done, said or not said, not only during my time with Marnie but even reviewing my time with Charlotte and noticing any similarities. I was doing this review as unemotionally and in a detached manner as I could, so I could get the big picture of what I had gone through to clearly see where I stood. Such dispassion didn't work perfectly, as you'll see later; a part of my mind was hijacked by emotions too strong to ignore. It was like there was a rebellious uprising going on in part of my brain, but I tried to push those feelings down or put them off till later until I could complete my review. What I saw wasn't a pretty picture.

I had crippled myself with my lack of self-esteem. It is true that I probably never had any, and as a kid that wasn't my fault, but I wasn't a kid anymore and I had still let that character flaw rule my life. Even when I had survived the first soul-murdering marriage, had learned to parent and make good independent decisions, had pulled my life and the lives of my kids back from the brink, and even had remade my physical body, still I thought I wasn't worth anything. I believed so completely that I wasn't whole unless I had somebody to love me (or, more accurately, someone who would allow me to obsess over her in a way I could call love) that I was willing to undergo torment after torment to make that happen. I had even sacrificed my children's happiness in the name of this love, deluding myself that it was partially for my kids, who "needed a mother." I had introduced a duplicitous gift horse into our family unit as surely as the Greeks did with the Trojans. She looked beautiful on the outside, but when that hidden trapdoor opened, out poured nothing but destruction.

Even worse, of course, was the feeling of shame that I had let it all happen again.

You would have thought that those years of horror with Charlotte had taught me enough to have avoided that same trap, but they obviously hadn't. Perhaps I had been so buffeted and beaten that I couldn't pay attention to anything more than just crawling out of there alive and pulling my kids out after me. Maybe I had used up every ounce of reserve I had and was truly broken in spirit beyond repair. Could it be that I never had any spirit in the first place? No backbone? No balls at all? Was I really a coward, less than a man, not worth the space I took up on the planet?

Or was I so selfish that I had seen something I wanted in Marnie and was willing to run over anything standing in my way of getting that—including my own kids? I was convinced, of course, that I was a terrible judge of character. "Fool me once, shame on you. Fool me twice, shame on me" certainly rang true in my life. But if I was such a bad judge, were all my instincts—including those newly formed ones I developed after Charlotte—also wrong? Was I just an all-around failure as a person, a parent, a man? Self-doubt reared up like a mythical dragon and I didn't know if I had it in me to slay it.

I now know, having learned things over the years, that I and all the kids were suffering from post-traumatic stress disorder, never resolved after surviving our experiences with Charlotte. According to the National Institute of Mental Health, some of the symptoms of the disorder in young children are bed-wetting and being unable to talk; and for older kids, becoming disrespectful or disruptive and exhibiting dangerous behaviors. I cringed when I thought back to Aaron's being unable to speak, Ethan's lashing out with fists and feet, and Lauren on that roof.

For adults, although we think of PTSD as causing flashbacks, it can in fact cause difficulty remembering details or feelings about the traumatic events. In my case, I think it caused me to have trouble noticing or acknowledging any warning signs about Marnie that showed she was enough like Charlotte in so many ways, they could have been twins. The disorder also causes negative thoughts about oneself (check) and distorted feelings of guilt or blame (check and check). I felt guilty about what I had put the kids through and blamed myself for all the things that had befallen us.

I was a walking textbook example of all of the above and didn't even know it. My lack of self-knowledge was stunning.

I didn't tie myself to a shrink or counselor because, although many people find them helpful, I wasn't one of those people. That may have been from the fact that I had trouble even accessing my own feelings after shutting them down for so long, and therefore didn't give the professionals much to work with, or it may have partially been that I was resentful of all the times I had been coerced to go see psychologists during my court fight with Charlotte. But whatever the reason, or combination of reasons, I was going to go this alone and I set out to do just that.

I wasn't sleeping well (another symptom of PTSD), so I used that time and the times I was exercising to devote to sorting out my past actions. This was my own attempt at the meditation recommended by many well-meaning friends (who may have feared I was going to have a nervous breakdown wading through this hell again). I thought long and hard and tried to see myself with brutal honesty. I shed some tears for my kids and myself (this, as it turned out, may have been my form of prayer) and, when I was done with this rigorous self-examination, I did the only thing I could think of: I called my children all together and apologized to them.

I told them how sorry I was for all that they had to endure because of my ignorance and blindness. I apologized for all my poor decisions and the times I hadn't defended or protected them. I told them how I had tried very hard to relive all that had gone before, so I could kick over every rock and see what lay beneath them. I cited incidences I recalled about each of them and invited them to tell me what they remembered, what they had suffered, and what still hurt. Then I apologized for those things.

We talked and cried and then I witnessed a miracle—they forgave me! This wasn't just lip service, like when adults toss off an easy "It's okay." They meant it, and it humbled me. I was astonished at the people they had become. After all they had been through, they were still able to be open and forgiving and generous of spirit. What had I ever done to deserve to share my life with such wonderful people?

I mentally whispered, Thank you, God to a god I didn't yet believe in as we all hugged each other. Since then we have never let go.

Everything wasn't us singing "Kumbaya" right off the bat, however. Lauren, who may have been the most damaged by my relationship with Marnie, was already out of the house and building a very independent life without me (she had stayed close to her siblings during the whole ordeal, and I credit that relationship with holding the family together when I seemed unable to keep it from floundering on the rocks). She was glad Marnie was gone and admitted she had been angry with me for what she saw as my taking Marnie's side against her, but she was willing to listen when I explained how I was just trying to keep Marnie from adding even more to the abuse heaped on her. Lauren said she understood no one was perfect, everyone made mistakes, and that the anger she felt about me had eventually dissipated.

Emily was very glad to have me "back," as she put it, and Abigail said she always knew I loved her and all the siblings. I had just been caught in a bad situation. She said they had all (except for Lauren) been fooled by Marnie, not just me, and now that she was gone, everything was going to be better. None of them ever used the phrase "Now everything will go back to normal," and good thing, since our "normal" had been pretty warped.

The boys were much less verbal about the whole thing, although Aaron, by this time, had learned to speak a little more often (his words are still sparse, to this day). Ethan spit out that he had been very "pissed off" at Marnie and all her family, and he had felt like punching the brother more than once. Aaron said he was particularly sorry that Lauren had gotten so hurt in all of this, and that he too was really glad those people were out of our lives for good.

Me too.

As I rebuilt the relationships with all of my children, I learned that looking for love in all the wrong places meant looking for it outside of myself. There was no woman who was going to fill that hole in my soul I had carried around my whole life. Nor could I fill it with food. I couldn't even fill it with too much work. Nothing external was going to work for me, so I decided to try the internal. I would restrict myself to working on helping my children, and would build up my own self-esteem at the same time.

I just wasn't sure where to begin.

When Marnie had left our bedroom, and moved into the one with her mother and brother, I was left alone and with lots of time to turn over in my mind how things had gone so wrong—again. I had no one to talk to about the situation. (In truth, I was too embarrassed to speak about it with anyone. How could I have been such a schmuck all over again?)

Sifting through my life and actions to see my part in creating and sustaining two such disastrous marriages was hard work. Facing the harm I had done my children was a painful chore too, but I knew it was important and I pressed on.

I had to fight through a sea of resentment, and those dark waters almost drowned me. Instead of a clear and flowing stream, I discovered I was living in a stagnant sink where the drain was blocked, and no guilt, blame, or shame could run out. The clog preventing such clearing was resentment. I was awash in it.

I literally shook with anger over Marnie and her family—especially her brother. I couldn't rid myself of the mental picture of that giant violent man raising a fist to strike Emily. That scene was burned into my retina, and it was before my eyes every day. I could turn my thoughts to healthier channels, but just like a river whose channel has been rerouted, I would always come right back to that same course, that burning resentment.

He had scared my little girl. He had threatened her physically. He had added to her pain and trauma. He had assaulted her as surely as if his fist had landed on her cheek.

Leader of the Pack

I wanted him dead.

I not only wanted him dead, I wanted him dead slowly and painfully and at my hands. He became my new obsession, and no amount of willpower could shake that feeling. I found myself constructing elaborate fantasies of how I would kill him.

I rehearsed scenarios of murder until I had one as sharp as a well-honed blade. I wanted to kill him with my bare hands. I would neutralize his height and weight advantage (he was 6 feet, 4 inches tall and 230 pounds, and I was considerably smaller and lighter). I would make use of my karate training and strike him just below his knee. This would snap it, breaking the ligaments, and drop him like a stone. I would use a hard-downward force and keep moving toward him as he fell. With my opposite hand, I would hit him at the bottom of his nose, using the heel of my hand to drive his nose bone right back into his brain. This move would kill him painfully and quickly, but not so quickly that he couldn't see my eyes as he hit the ground. My eyes would be the last things he'd ever see.

They say that resentment is like drinking poison and waiting for the other person to die, and I found that to be true. I was eaten up with my need for revenge.

My thoughts became a team of wild horses, and I could no longer rein them in. Try as I might, I was losing the fight and about to spin out of control. I was unable to harness my thoughts, but there was Someone who wasn't powerless, and I was about to meet Him.

CHAPTER 13
GOD WITH SKIN

There's an old saying that all of us entertain angels unawares. We don't see or can't acknowledge that we have been sent help to get over some of the big bumps in life we can't handle alone. God, it seems, does for us what we can't do for ourselves. I had been the recipient of such a gift, but hadn't recognized it as such.

The nannies were two angels sent to be of service to me. Looking back, that was as plain as the nose on my face. (In fact, my employee Idan, who suggested hiring them, had the shadow of wings on his back too.)

Jessica, despite the fact that she couldn't stay for the long haul, also was an angel in disguise, teaching me a healthy way to love and be loved. She gave me a space to heal my heart and stop the hemorrhage caused by my time with Charlotte.

But the higher power had also been setting me up for this time in my life when I would be struggling with overpowering resentment (and losing the struggle). He had sent in reinforcements even before the battle had been joined. It's as though there was a whole cavalry waiting in the woods for the signal to rush in and join the fight.

Remember the mezuzah Shira had insisted I put on the doorframe of our house to give blessings to everyone who enters? And recall how the rabbi and his little girl had come to the door and seen the mezuzah, and the child had no longer been frightened because her father had pointed out that the mezuzah's presence meant they were at the home of a friend? I didn't know I was a friend to the rabbi and the people of his congregation yet. I didn't know I had spiritually joined that community by donating the clothes to needy young couples. I thought that when I turned away the rabbi's invitation to visit his Chabad synagogue and closed the door, I had made a decision. No religion for me. I was joining no congregation.

I was wrong.

God decided it was time to tell that cavalry to charge. I needed help from my people—even if I didn't know they were my people at the time.
***
It wasn't surprising I didn't recognize that God had been knocking at my door when I turned down the rabbi's invitation all those years before. I

knew nothing about being a Jew. The first (and only) time I'd ever been in a synagogue was for a cousin's bar mitzvah, and I'd had to borrow a yarmulke. I was glad it wasn't like the Christian services I'd attended, in which everyone seemed to know the words and all the song lyrics (though I could belt out a mean Christmas carol or two myself). In the temple, though some people were up on the "altar" (bimah) bowing and chanting (in Hebrew, a language I knew only from watching Ben Hur), nobody in the congregation seemed to be paying much attention. Everyone was holding conversations like we were on the subway. They shut up only when the kid whose bar mitzvah it was got up to read his part. It gave me good cover for the fact that I had no idea what I should be doing. I shook hands, kissed cheeks, handed over a check, and got the hell out of there.

But Marnie was a Sephardic Jew and had wanted to go to synagogue, at least on the High Holidays, so I went with her. I had even sent my kids to a reform (Jew "lite") temple over the years so they could get some connection to a Jewish community, and they all had their bar and bat mitzvahs.

Don't get me wrong; I didn't go all Jewish Holy Roller after my marriage to Marnie ended. I was too cautious and truly too cynical to turn true believer. But I got to be less of a stranger to other Jews, and they to me. I didn't feel like such an outsider anymore. Little by little, I came to accept and feel more comfortable in my Jewishness. As it is said, "I opened my fist one tiny grudging bit, and miracles happened."

But that was still down the road a ways. So, there I was, doing battle with resentment and losing. The noise of my hatred was drowning out all other sounds—of gratitude, self-discovery, spiritual transformation—and I was getting very tired and depleted. Then the horn sounded, and from the left flank that waiting cavalry charged.

I was on a plane coming back from a long weekend in Florida. I had taken four of the kids (Lauren was away for the summer in Spain) to escape the horrors of that house with Marnie and her family. To pass the time, I fell into conversation with a guy in the seat next to me. Why it is sometimes easier to talk to total strangers about personal things is beyond me (though I imagine that is the premise behind the confessional for Catholics, where they spill all intimate details to the unseen priest behind a partition in the darkened stall). But whatever the reason (and I now know that reason—again with the divine coincidences), I started to tell him my life story.

Perhaps I was just overflowing with feelings and needed a pot in which to pour them, but I told him about Charlotte and what had happened with Marnie. I confided how guilty and full of shame I was for what I had done to my children. I even revealed (in less gory detail than in my imaginings) how I wanted revenge on Marnie and her family.

The man was a good listener and, at the end of my recitation of woe, he offered no empty platitudes or feel-good pop psychology. He only suggested something that had helped him in his life.

He was an Orthodox Jew from Monsey, New York. He also followed a worldwide Jewish outreach organization called Aish HaTorah. As part of its mission to spread the wisdom of Judaism, Aish sends out to anyone who subscribes free daily emails of Jewish wisdom, affirmations, proverbs, and Torah teachings. These are short affirmations and pieces of wisdom that he thought might be helpful to me. No hard sell, no pushing of religion, no conversion necessary—just a helpful suggestion that I should check out the Aish daily email when I got home.

I did just that.

I went to Aish.com and entered my email address. Almost immediately, one of the Aish affirmations arrived in my email. Here is what I read:

When we've been wronged, it is very difficult to overcome feelings of animosity and revenge. As the saying goes, "revenge is sweeter than honey." It takes great strength of character to overcome the natural desire for revenge and instead to forget the entire matter and remove it from one's heart as if it had never occurred.

Such a level is easy only for angels who do not have normal human emotions, but not for ordinary mortals. Nevertheless, the Torah states this obligation explicitly: "Do not hate your brother in your heart. Do not take revenge and do not bear a grudge."
(Leviticus 19:17,8)

Today, ask yourself: Is there anyone toward whom I feel resentment, animosity, or a grudge? If yes, imagine being able to let those feelings melt away. Experience yourself being free from the burden of those heavy feelings. Forgive!!! Allow yourself to feel the relief and lightness of living in the present—totally free from those counterproductive thoughts and feelings.
Rabbi Moshe Chaim Luzzatto - Path of the Just

I immediately thought, I've been set up!

The man on the plane had obviously told the site's webmaster my story, and he had chosen this particular entry to speak directly to my circumstances. The reading had been customized specifically to me, to reel me in or get me to make a contribution or something.

After a few minutes of wild speculation, I calmed down and realized that such a paranoid supposition couldn't be true. I hadn't given my email to the man on the plane. He had no way of knowing if or when I gave my email address to Aish.com. It really was just a coincidence.

I went back and read the entry again, and something happened. I felt something almost like a stirring inside of me—an absolute knowing that the words contained in it were true; true for me, true for everyone. In my inability to give up the resentment I felt for Marnie's family, I had been left with immovable negative emotions—anger, resentment, hostility, even hatred.

I knew too that the hatred would calcify, making me unable to move forward in my life, but forgiveness? The reading spoke of forgiveness.

Would I be able to actually forgive those people? It seemed too tall an order.

I pondered the words of the reading for days. They had infiltrated my brain just as thoroughly as the thoughts of resentment had taken it over before this. But by crowding out the resentment, room was being made for a new pattern of thought, a new channel for the clear water of the spirit to flow—a channel carved by forgiveness.

I'd need a river guide for this one.

I went back to Aish.com and began to wander around. The site was a huge compendium of everything anyone would ever need to know about Judaism: the history of its people; why the various traditions had come into being; answers about observing Shabbat, the High Holidays, and all the other special days of the Jewish calendar; Torah readings and discussions; a section on spirituality, another on handling family matters; and an Ask the Rabbi section with thousands of questions asked by people just like me, answered with patience and wisdom. I read stories of hope and inspiration from other Jews around the world and slowly, bite by bite, I even digested the section entitled Judaism 101.

I discovered that Aish HaTorah had been founded by Rabbi Noah Weinberg, nearly 40 years before, with a mission: to help Jews study the Torah and, through such study, not only discover themselves but fulfill what he believed was their mission, which was to save the world. The rabbi also felt that the Jewish people were in danger of being lost to history through ignorance of their own religion and via the assimilation of Jews marrying outside their faith and raising their children as non-Jews. He thought that by educating Jews and making such teachings readily available to Jews everywhere, the tide could be stemmed, and our people reclaimed. I realized after reading the site for a few weeks that I had, in fact, begun to think of my fellow Jews as "our" people.

When I read on the site "Life isn't about finding yourself, it is about creating yourself," I knew they were talking right to me.

I began to read up on the subject of forgiveness. It took some time for the words to be anything more than a foreign language to me, but eventually the light permeated even this thick skull of mine. Here's some of what I read:

When asked for forgiveness, a Jew is enjoined to forgive. This can be the hardest act of all. After all, we may have been grievously hurt, in body, mind, or heart. To forgive is tantamount to executing a divine function....

Nothing more quickly procures divine forgiveness for our sins, both those we remember and those we don't, than forgiving those who have sinned against us. When we stand before God on Rosh Hashanah and Yom Kippur, our most compelling defense is: "I have forgiven those who sinned against me. Please forgive me in turn."

Every time we forgive, we open up the gates of forgiveness in the world. And we are the first ones to walk through.

When we forgive others, we help ourselves as much as we help those whom we forgive. We are elevating ourselves and will feel much better when we forgive than if we would keep on adding more and more resentment.

People on the highest level explicitly state each night before they go to sleep that they forgive anyone who insulted them, even if those people will not ask for forgiveness on their own.

I had been rehearsing my resentments against Marnie's family over and over, like a daily mantra, and I began to see that doing so gave the resentments energy and kept them alive. It started to dawn on me that by dropping the resentments, I would finally be able to unchain myself from that horrible family.

Forgiving them would set me free.

But the one reading on forgiveness that really got to me was this one: "When someone hurts you, find the lesson in the hurt and then learn how to apply that lesson to others that have been hurt."

I had learned some tough lessons. I did know how to survive many things that might help other single fathers out there: harsh judges, ignorant bureaucrats, abusive cops, interfering "well-wishers," bad spouses, physical violence, and emotional abuse. I had suffered them all and was still standing, so perhaps those lessons I had found from my being hurt could be used to help others. I would have to think about it. (I didn't yet know God already had thought about it and would present me with my marching orders shortly.)

Aish.com also taught me that I needn't be discouraged by the obstacles and difficulties of my life. There were others who had shared the same pain and would help me shoulder the burdens.

The word aish means "fire" and I would, over the years, meet many of the people of Aish and recognize the divine spark in myself by seeing the divine spark in each of them.

They were literally "God with skin."

As I delved more into the teachings on Aish.com, my sense of isolation, as well as my twin weights of guilt and shame, began to lift. My focus started to shift away from thoughts of revenge, anger, and pain and turned instead toward a future that suddenly seemed wider and accessible.

Things appeared less bleak in my world, and the kids, amazingly, seemed to have survived and even thrived despite my mistakes. My vision had become distorted by guilt, but blaming myself only made me want to close my eyes to the truth of the situation, and flying blind was no way to live a life.

I began reading a book that the man on the plane had recommended:

Gateway to Happiness, by Zelig Pliskin. The book encouraged me to actively search out the good things in life, to view life through a lens of gratitude.

Now it would be great to report that I practiced all of this perfectly and got so spiritual I practically levitated, but that isn't true. I tried to do what was suggested, and when I became even a bit open to the idea that gratitude could make a difference in my life, I realized my perception of things both outside of me and inside of me was changing.

Even I, lowly man that I was, had a wealth of treasure inside of me and, despite it all, it was still shining there. Better still, this focus on gratitude kept most of my consciousness focused on listening to the angels of my nature, instead of the devils poking me with their pitchforks.

It is a simple fact that the human brain can't entertain more than one thought at a time, so I realized I should make sure the thought taking up my brain was one of positivity. I began with the notion to be grateful every single day—especially for all the love around me.

I had a little trouble with the idea of God, so I had some resistance to overcome when it came to being grateful...grateful to whom?

I decided that question was too large for me to ponder. I would try just being grateful in general—like a radio tower broadcasting a signal. It wasn't my concern who received the signal. It was just my responsibility to keep broadcasting.

So, since I was charged with being grateful for all the love surrounding me, I started with those directly around me—my children. I made an effort to tell my kids I loved them, gave them hugs, patted their shoulders or backs, noticed (and make a big deal of) their victories, and was sad with them over their defeats. I didn't walk on eggshells around them; I just tried to notice the good things and shut up about most of the criticisms. I treated them like the precious things they are to me, and how we dealt with each other started to change.

Since I was trying to celebrate the joys, both big and small, I used the time during my daily runs to be aware of where I was and what I could be thankful for in that moment. I tried to be grateful for the sun on my face or the shade of the trees on a hot day. At meals, I was grateful for the food and for the money I made to pay for groceries.

I realized that material things didn't provide happiness (so I reluctantly took my BMW off the list). My true treasure was always going to be found within and in those I loved who surrounded me.

When a negative thought intruded on my thinking, I quickly substituted it for a positive one. If I got stuck on adding to what I now thought of as my Gratitude List, I used the alphabet. I started with "A" for air, since I was happy I was still breathing. "B" was for the bravery it took for me to serve those papers on Marnie and make a start toward freeing us from that mess. "C" was easy—"C" was for my children, each one worth more than I could calculate…and I slowly made my way on through to "Z."

The insomnia that plagued me during the last few years with Marnie took a while to leave me (it is part of the "flight or fight" reflex built into humans to ensure that enough adrenaline was pumped to have kept primitive man from getting eaten by a saber-toothed tiger…or modern man from getting killed by an ex-wife). When the insomnia finally left me, it left behind a gift: I now need only five hours sleep to be fully rested. Bonus! But before I was relieved of the insomnia, I used the gratitude alphabet trick late at night while I was trying to fall asleep. It was like counting spiritual sheep.

After a while, marking things worthy of my gratitude became second nature, a reflex, like shading my eyes from bright light—very important but unnoticed. It became a part of me.

I began to feel the weight of blame and guilt lift from my shoulders.

The people I met through Aish HaTorah believed deeply in the power of the Jewish people to change the world, to steer it on a course of sanity and true liberation. I needed such a course set for my own journey. Everything to them was one seamless page in the incredible unfolding story of Jewish history. I was to take my place in that history and through it, help reclaim my life.

CHAPTER 14
SPIRITUALITY "R" US

I go way too fast for a normal human; I always have. Tending to a zillion details for work, sorting hundreds of emails in the time it takes most people just to open theirs, sleeping only half as much as everybody else (not falling asleep until 2 a.m. even though I am up with the sun). Relaxation is not in my makeup, nor is making time to study a subject.

If I had to learn religion the old-fashioned way, the teachers and rabbis would have lost me as a pupil right away.

But the bumper stickers' sayings, easily digestible little bits of wisdom, and pint-size profundities suited me just fine, and I began to grow spiritually, despite myself. I started to see there were no coincidences and that all those things that had happened to me, no matter how painful, were all parts of a jigsaw puzzle—one-piece fitting to the next—in perfect order, presented when I was able to see where the piece belonged.

It certainly seemed, at times, as though I had been given more than I could handle, and yet I hadn't been. Adversity had stretched my skills as a parent and my soul as a human being. I was a better man for having gone through everything, and saw that the Divine had intervened as necessary for me to get where I was going. Better still, He was butting right into my kid's lives as well. I noticed my children were getting better. They were laughing more, talking over one another at the table, poking one another, and sassing me back. They lost that beaten-dog look. The sun came out again, for all of us, and I knew that many of the healing rays were coming out of a new spiritual journey.

There was a bigger picture being revealed to me too. I was being fed faith one teaspoonful at a time, so I wouldn't choke on it. It was nourishment just the same.
***

I was running the big camera store I had reinvented our distribution business from, and one day in walked a young man named Seth. He was soliciting donations of cameras and equipment for a project called Artists4Israel, which sent graffiti artists to Israel to decorate bomb shelters. This was to make the shelters more visible and raise awareness that when bombs fell, they fell on Jews, Arabs, and Christians alike. The project also served as a way for "influencers" (the young urban graffiti artists themselves) to see for themselves what a wonderful country Israel was and bring that knowledge back to the States with them.

I happily donated the things he needed and asked him to be sure to come tell me how it went when he returned. When he did, reporting that the project was a smashing success, we put our heads together to set up a fundraiser to help raise money for the following year's project. (He arranged to have a fantastic 3D mural painted on the side of my store to thank me, which once again shows you that the more good you put out, the more good comes back to you.)

At that fundraiser, I met a wonderful gentleman named Charles Rothberg, and we struck up a friendship. At dinner a few months later, we were exchanging stories about our lives as usual, and Charles shared a small problem he was having and asked my advice about which way to go with it. With all the fervor of converts everywhere, I whipped out a little of my new found Aish.com-supplied wisdom, which I thought addressed his need perfectly. I was a little taken aback when he laughed.

"What is funny about that?" I said. "It's from the Torah. I got it from a daily email subscription service I have sent from a site called Aish.com."

"Oh, I know where you got it, Matt," Charles said, and took a business card from his wallet. It read "Charles Rothberg, Chairman of the Board of Directors, Aish Center in New York." That was New York City's branch of Aish HaTorah.

Talk about coincidences!

I told Charles how much Aish.com had helped me and that I hadn't missed a day reading those all-important emails. I said that I finally felt connected to Judaism and to a community. I may not have admitted it out loud, but I certainly had been feeling it for a while—the lessons I was learning on Aish.com sounded very much like the voice of God to me. The wisdom those little sayings and readings contained was divinely inspired, I was sure of it. They resonated in me like the ringing of a bell and awakened something in me—a thirst for learning; a yearning to be among my fellows, to be part of a community, and to be a better man and father.

He was, of course, delighted that an organization so dear to his heart was helping his friend. He asked if I wanted to learn more about Judaism with one of the Aish rabbis. I could ask any questions I had and study any facet of Judaism I wanted and, best of all, such conversations would be one on one and the rabbi would come to me! That sounded like it would fit into my ever-busy life, so I agreed. Rabbi Elijah Roth came out to my place of business in New York for the first of many meetings (and great conversations) we had together. Aish had a group of such rabbis who would go out to educate businessmen and women about Judaism as part of a project called the Aish Executive Learning Program. Rabbi Roth and I began our talks on the subject of free will. Our conversation went something like this:

Humans are like God in the sense that we have free will. 'Free will' does not mean picking chocolate over vanilla. That's simply a preference, just as a cow chooses to eat hay instead of grass.

Rather, 'free will' refers to decisions that are uniquely human: a moral choice to do right or wrong. This stems from the divine soul that is unique to all human beings.

There are times when you know objectively that something is good for you, but your physical desires get in the way and distort your outlook. The animal soul within us wants to choose the easy path, which may not be the morally correct choice. Sometimes we can actually hear ourselves fighting it out.

Here's a conversation you may have had with yourself:

Divine soul: "Let's get out of bed early today and really accomplish something meaningful!"
Animal soul: "Leave me alone; I'd rather sleep."
Divine soul: "Come on, let's be great!"
Animal soul: "Relax. What's the big deal if we wait till tomorrow?"

What's going on? Are you schizophrenic? No, just battling opposing sides within yourself. And that's what makes the human being so unique. Of all God's creatures, only humans can become elevated through choice, as we are not bound in our decisions by any pre-ordained laws. That's truly divine.

The rabbi and I had many conversations about making moral decisions in one's life, which in turn led to other philosophical discussions on a wide range of topics. With each conversation, I felt my soul expanding, and I began to see life as though through a new pair of glasses.

Over the next year or so, the rabbi helped me learn more about being a Jew and an ethical man. He was bolstered in this by my continued reading of the wisdom on Aish.com. Some of the entries touched me deeply, like these:

The Joy of Virtue Is Its Own Reward
Even if a person would receive no other reward besides the joy and pleasure he has from performing a good deed, it would be sufficient. The greatest potential for pleasure is the pleasure we experience when performing a good deed.

***

A just person may fall seven times and rise (Proverbs 24:16)
"I should have known better from last time," one says.
Some lessons are not learned so easily, even from experience. We may understand something with our intellect, yet it may not have filtered down into our hearts.
Today I shall try to maintain faith in myself even when I make the same mistake over and over again.

***

The Jewish approach to suffering is that everything happens for the good, but we are finite and cannot see the whole picture.
We trust God and say, "I haven't yet figured out why, but God knows this is for the best."

***

Everything Is for the Best
All the Almighty does is for your benefit. When you know that in your heart, you will not be broken or become sad regardless of how the Almighty sets up your life. You will accept whatever happens with love.

***

And, if I am ever tempted to slide back into my old need for revenge for the wrongs done to me or my children, I need only reference this reading:

Revenge
The Torah states explicitly: "Do not hate your brother in your heart. Do not take revenge and do not bear a grudge." (Leviticus 19:17)
Imagine being able to let those feelings melt away. Forgive! Allow yourself to feel the relief and lightness of living in the present—totally free

from those counterproductive thoughts and feelings.

***

Over the time period in which our once-a-week meetings took place, I not only got to know Judaism on a deep and spiritual level, but Rabbi Roth got to know me. He heard my story, saw my growth, and understood that I was trying to share all the beauty and depth I found in the religion of our forefathers with my children. He soon surprised me with an announcement. Because of what he saw in me, I was to be awarded The Jewish Continuity Award by the Aish Center. Here's what the award means according to the inscription: "The Jewish Continuity Award celebrates individuals committed to imparting Jewish wisdom to the next generation, and who are passionate about Jewish education and values, both within their community and personal lives."

I was proud to accept the award and share the story of my journey homeward to Judaism with hundreds of invited guests and all five of my children. It was a profound honor.

Soon after, I was asked first to assist with a gala (like the one where I had been given my Jewish Continuity Award) and then to serve on Aish's board of directors to help them fulfill their mission of helping Jews discover or deepen their knowledge of and ties to Judaism. My "get it done" talents and enthusiasm, coupled with my dramatic story and recent experience, would be of great benefit to the Aish Center, Rabbi Roth felt. Since Aish is an organization devoted to promoting Judaism among Jews, I was the perfect poster child. I, who had never learned any Hebrew, who had never even had a Bar Mitzvah, had finally come home to my people, my heritage, and my faith.

I was planning to refuse the seat on the board, as I had just sold my business and wanted time to enjoy my less-busy life and take stock of where I was and what I had learned. But, as always, God had a different plan. Before I could even turn the position down, I was offered another—this time as chairman of the board of directors, to fill a vacancy that had suddenly become available due to the unexpected stepping down of the previous board chairman (the person who had succeeded Charles). This had left the board in quite a bind, and they needed my help immediately.

(I could almost hear God laughing, saying, "I'm sorry to interrupt, Matt. You were saying how you couldn't find time to help my other children because you were too busy?"

I knew better than to argue with The Boss, and I became chairman of

116

the board of directors of the Aish Center. I also filled another position at Aish, that of assisting the man in charge of fundraising for Aish. He was Rabbi Noah Weinberg's right-hand man while the rabbi lived, and has raised tens of millions of dollars for Aish in Jerusalem. I have learned a lot from him and am delighted to help raise money to continue this vital mission. I have even been lucky enough to travel the world on trips to promote Aish and the wonderful work it does in spreading the word to the Jewish diaspora.

I had known nothing of Judaism. My parents had changed their last name to assimilate. I hadn't even been taught the Yiddish that they spoke in our home. I donned the big red suit and acted the part of Santa Claus at college for the math department's holiday party. I married a woman who was a nominal Jew, but together we sent out holiday cards with photos of our family dressed in holly-motif sweaters with a fully decorated Christmas tree in the background. My children knew nothing of their Jewish heritage until the arrival of our nannies, and I didn't even know what a mezuzah was until introduced to the custom by Shira. All the rich history and tradition of our faith had been foreign to me, and I hadn't even noticed the lack until after that hole in my soul was filled. From that day to this, I truly have come a long way, baby.

Now I know there are no divine coincidences. God did have a plan for me. It just unfolded slowly. I would have missed it if it had been any faster. The Almighty followed His schedule and, as always, He was right on time.

Many blessings disguised as tragedies have occurred in my life, and I now know I was spared from death not only to experience them but to share them with others. Had I not lived through the despair and pain and entertained those suicidal and murderous thoughts caused by the horrific circumstances I and my family had survived, I would never have found this connection with my faith and my tribe. I needed to be bent, but never broken, in order for my Creator to mold me into the shape most useful to His purpose.

Once a blind, anguished, and tormented man stumbling alone through life, I have been granted sight and given a map and a helping hand whenever I needed it. That old saying "When the student is ready, the teacher will appear" applied to me and still does, but now I am one of the teachers. No one is more surprised than I at this turn of events.

I know that I am a walking miracle.☐

CHAPTER 15
PUT ME IN, COACH

We had survived the tsunami and then the earthquake brought on by my terrible life choices, and I was grateful to still be standing. I was even more thankful that my kids were turning out all right. In the back of my head (and even more than most parents, I think), I expected at least one of them to become a drug addict, prostitute, or serial killer, after all they had been through. Imagine my surprise when each and every one of them came up shining like a star.

Lauren was a difficult teenager. She was 11 or 12 when I married her stepmother, Marnie. The marriage was particularly rough on Lauren because Marnie found it hard to tolerate anything or show compassion. This made her relationship with Lauren rocky even from the start. I tried to get Marnie to cut her some slack, saying Lauren was only a teenage girl going through some difficulties. But Marnie was jealous and wanted to be my sole focus (a fact she hid while we were dating. I should have seen the warning signs when she insisted we not speak of the kids during our dates. "This is our time together," she'd whine. "Let's make this 'us time' quality time"). I wasn't really allowed to voice my opinion about this (or as time went on, about anything, without risking an all-out war. It often felt to me like I was gasping for air. I can only imagine how the children felt.

The smallest disagreement with Marnie and there was a screaming scene. Lauren spent lots of time trying to defend herself and retaliating against Marnie's harsh treatment of her. Lauren had taken charge of the house after the nannies left, and her position must have threatened Marnie. She was a strong young woman and used what she could to fight back. She would invite her friends over to taunt Marnie.

Lauren and I had a rocky relationship too, and I had tiptoed around her in the past, scared she would say something to the custody evaluator. It was not the greatest foundation for a healthy relationship with one's child, and adding Marnie to the scene was like adding fuel to the fire. Whenever I tried to intervene, I made things worse. I justified my backing off by convincing myself that Lauren was strong and independent and would be all right. And I knew there was no convincing Marnie to back off without increasing her wrath aimed at my kids and me.

Lauren was a super student athlete (captain both varsity field hockey and lacrosse teams. I used to sneak out of work to watch her games) and graduated high school with a 4.3 grade-point average as a National AP Scholar. I wanted her to go to SUNY, but though she was offered a full-ride scholarship, she chose to go instead to a top tier private school in the Midwest. She studied communications and Spanish and works for a Fortune top-20 company in corporate communications.

I was extremely surprised she turned out so well. It seemed to me I spent a lot of time grounding her as a teen for her fierce independence. She had detached from me early, and I parented her the least. Being a take-charge person and being in control helped her. In between my wives, Lauren organized things in the house, ordered the other kids around, and really asked for very little of my input.

We returned to having a closer relationship after Marnie was gone. By this time Lauren had graduated college and put away her anger toward me. I am very grateful for the wonderful relationship we share today. We have "parental" discussions about the other kids, all of whom (except for independent Ethan) will consult with Lauren about what moves to make in their lives. Lauren still, it should be said, offers Ethan her suggestions, like them or not, and they are always insightful ones.

Lauren has a good head on her shoulders; she is emotionally stable, centered, and focused. Sometimes she seems more mature than I do! She was my firstborn and my first to be married, and I am proud of whatever piece I contributed to helping her grow into the strong and confident woman that she is.

Ethan was a very happy baby, but when his mother started acting out, he was the child who took it the hardest. He was visibly upset by her behavior, and I think he never truly recovered from it. He was only 7 when she left, but he was the first of the children to understand she wasn't coming back. He turned a little wild and disobedient at first, but later grew closer to me.

One of the most telling scenes of his childhood was when he walked out on the court appointed social worker when Charlotte spouted negative garbage about me. He refused to ever go back, and he never saw his mother again.

It took Ethan a couple of years to find his balance and, though he was close to Yael and Shira, the rotation of female figures in his life was very upsetting. To him there was no stability, and it appears he had no one he could really count on. This exacerbated the normal hormonal teenage angst boys feel, and I had to often remind myself that raising a child is a marathon, not a sprint.

He and Marnie had gotten along brilliantly until she turned on him, and their relationship never recovered. There were some very low moments, and Ethan did take several stabs at trying to talk to me about it, but I wouldn't allow any bad-mouthing of Marnie. What I was doing was just making Ethan shove his feelings down. I figured taking him to karate and Devils games meant I was being a good dad, when actually I was letting him down.

Ethan was depressed and was doing poorly at school. His emotional issues led him to become as undermotivated as it gets, despite his being the most naturally academically gifted of all my children. To hell with his studies; he seemed devoted only to becoming the Nintendo Champion of the World. When he finally graduated high school, I breathed a big sigh of relief. He then got into Seton Hall University by the skin of his teeth. Without trying, he got straight A's in his Asian studies classes and was put into the honors program. True to form, Ethan dropped out after a year.

He came home and said college wasn't for him. He wanted to become an actor. These are not the words guaranteed to warm the cockles of a father's heart, but I decided right then and there that what Ethan needed was my love and support (while tentatively suggesting he get a degree in business or anything else as a backup). Not surprisingly, he ignored my suggestion.

So, Ethan went off to New York City to appear in handfuls of off-off Broadway showcases before he eventually moved to Los Angeles. He gave none of us in the family any indication of how he was faring in California, so when Abigail was looking at colleges, I took it as an excuse to visit Ethan under the guise of helping his sister check out some West Coast schools. What I saw alarmed me. Ethan was disheveled, and he looked like he was skipping way too many meals. He was living in a hostel and had no car. Things were not working out for him out there, but he hadn't wanted any of us to know that. Ethan wanted to become a success first.

I gave him money for food and convinced him to come back to the East Coast, saying, "I know people who know people. I can help you get a leg up in the theater world." He took that bait and moved back to my house, where I set him up in the basement with a comfortable bed and three-square meals a day (at least my version of "three hots and a cot" didn't include bars on the door). He combined going to auditions with being a car valet for a year.

I felt like I had made too many parental mistakes with Ethan and that he was going nowhere. I was very concerned and even discussed his situation with Lauren.

"He has to understand that he will have his own place to live, bills will come due, and he will need to find a way to pay them," I said.

Being able to stand on one's own two feet financially has always been a mark of adulthood for me, and I wanted my children to understand that.

I was strongly considering giving him the boot when the situation changed. Ethan asked me to dinner.

"We live together," I pointed out. "We have dinner together all the time."

"No," Ethan said. "You're a busy guy, and I want your complete attention."

I thought he was going to announce he was going to an acting school in Europe he had been interested in, so I planned my response.

"Let's switch roles," I'd say. "I'll go to acting school and you go run my camera store. If you were the father in this situation, what would you say to your son?"

It turns out I didn't have to use my prepared remarks. At the restaurant, with a self-satisfied smirk, Ethan pulled a paper out of his backpack and handed it to me. It was an acceptance letter from Columbia University! I admit I thought at first it was a fake and, knowing me as he did, Ethan quickly showed me the university's seal on the top. He had even gotten a call from the dean himself, saying that Ethan's essay had so impressed him that he was eager to welcome him to Columbia. I was ecstatic! It had been extremely painful to see my son not succeeding, and I was truly grateful that God had just reached down and saved Ethan. That cavalry had mounted up again.

Ethan said, "My dream was to be an actor, but I know what getting into Columbia means, so I am giving up my dream and going for it. I'm going to study political science."

Just as I was thanking God that he hadn't been diverted by getting into that European acting school, Ethan smiled a little wider and handed me another letter—this one accepting him into the Tisch School of the Arts at New York University!

We had a good father-son moment tossing that option back and forth. He had secretly auditioned and gotten in, and that acceptance validated his acting talent. All he had really needed was that validation and, having gotten it, he decided he couldn't pass up going to a school as prestigious as Columbia.

Ethan served an internship with a prominent political pundit while at Columbia, and now works for a pro-Israel organization, with the goal of changing the younger generation's views from being neutral or even opposing the support of Israel.

So, Ethan has become a political activist. He is helping people, achieving important things, and paying his own way. Ethan rose from the ashes of his own experiences. It is clear to me that it was divine intervention and another reminder that not all kids achieve on their parents' timeline. Ethan, despite his background, is very well adjusted and has made great use of his native intelligence and passion to make a difference in the world. What more could any man ask of a son?

Aaron is still running the big camera store I built. He is the general manager and oversees a staff of 15 people. He is back in school at a community college, where he plans to put in his two years before switching to a larger school. In his first year, he was a straight-A student. He had previously attended Drew University on a soccer scholarship, but had dropped out after only one semester, being neither fully verbal nor emotionally mature enough to handle the experience.

When he quit school, he just wanted to play video games in his room all day, but I insisted he have a job, though I wasn't willing to have him work in my company. I thought he was too irresponsible, so he got a job in a restaurant for a couple of years, where he was promoted to manager. Then I let him come to work for me. Aaron had started slowly but matured right in front of my eyes, and he began to learn what the real world was like. Now, at 26, he is finally ready for college, though he is unsure what he wants to study and needs to "find himself."

This, I'm sure, is a continuing reaction to the kind of trauma he went through when his mom left. The experience set him back. I had taken him out of the therapy he went to when his mother abandoned us. He was only 5 at the time, and the shrinks had tried play therapy with him. He learned to be one of the best ball bouncers at the practice, but he still didn't talk. The doctor called him "the strong, silent type" and, for the amount of money and commitment of time we were putting in, I needed to see better results than that.

Aaron is possessed of a winning smile, and he was and is very cute; both things got him out of a lot of trouble. He never had been a great student in school. Truth be told, he and Ethan had me worried for a while there. I was concerned, particularly about Aaron—that he doesn't become a total loser. Ethan developed those political skills, enabling him to take on and take out any opponent, but it was unclear for a while what Aaron might develop. When Aaron graduated with that outstanding soccer ability that had pulled him through, I felt a great sense of relief. When he got into college on the soccer scholarship, I felt the whole plan had worked. He has a little ADHD (like his dad), but soccer did keep him out of trouble.

Aaron is a great guy. He is the sibling whom all my other kids love. With his affable and likable personality, no one can stay mad at him for long, but he is not a people-pleaser. He is naturally charming but walks to the beat of his own drum. He has a girlfriend, who is also quite introverted but not too introspective, so she and Aaron seem to get along fine (even if it appears they must communicate telepathically, as neither one speaks much).

I have faith that Aaron's future will turn out fine and according to God's plan. I don't need to know the specifics—Aaron's other Father has got it covered.

When Charlotte left the house, it seemed the three older kids retreated under my wing (except for Lauren), but Emily was cared for largely by Yael. It was a natural fit. Emily is the gentlest and most compassionate of the kids.

She had been the weeper and had often thrown herself on the ground sobbing, but when her mom finally left, she came into her own a bit. She was little, only 4, and quickly adjusted, getting on so well with Yael that my some of my fears were alleviated.

As she grew, she was very well behaved and good at school. When she was about 9, I married Marnie, and Emily had the advantage, at least at the beginning, of being my second wife's favorite. Marnie treated her very nicely, and even when the abuse began, Emily was spared at first. When the behavior changed and Marnie turned on all the kids, Emily was crushed and took to her room to hide.

She tried to draw no attention to herself, but she was a natural star. In high school, she got picked to go to China to study as part of a national security language initiative. She was one of only 24 kids from across the country chosen for that. She also won the top foreign language award and now speaks fluent Mandarin. She attended the Elliott School of International Affairs at George Washington University in Washington, DC, where she graduated in three and a half years, magna cum laude, with a BA in international relations. She now works as a consultant in the DC area.

She is thoughtful and caring, and I can't take full credit for that. I believe how a child turns out is one-third genetics, one-third environment (parenting, friends, and others who nurture him or her), and one-third God's decision for a person's life. Emily was the easiest to raise, because really all she required was love and attention, and it was easy as a parent to give her both.

I did tend to give the oldest child at home the most attention as he or she became ready to get launched into adult life. When it came time for Emily to take that slot, Marnie had just left and I was able to truly give Emily all my attention. I helped her with her SAT; we visited colleges; I closely monitored her grades. It was like a loving assault by me, but it wasn't unwelcome. I had experience and good sense. Emily was driven and wanted to do well. Together we were determined to turn her life into something wonderful, and it appears we have.

All my girls were expected to achieve their full potential. I treated them no differently than I did the boys. They weren't allowed to consider getting married as their only option, nor were they going to live on a futon in my basement. In fact, how it turned out is that my girls are the ones poised to have the big corporate jobs in life, and I think that is great.

It is true that one's children are never fully launched. My children all still rely on me—even Lauren, who must be considered the one closest to being fully launched. She is 29, and we came together two years ago to celebrate her wedding in Israel. She was a beautiful bride and is now a full-grown and competent woman, but you never outgrow fatherhood.

Abigail, whom I continue to call "Munchkin" and probably will until the end of my life, is the youngest and therefore was the least affected by her mother's leaving. She has very little memory of Charlotte, and she is unsure if the memories she does have are real or just things she has been reminded of by someone else.

She was raised in those early years largely by the nannies and me. She was, and is, my baby, even though she now has reached the ripe old age of 21. She was the one most exposed to my parenting and for the longest time, so I am particularly proud of how she is coming along. She and Lauren have similar personalities—they are both hard workers, driven, and accomplished. Abigail might even be considered a tad aggressive sometimes, a trait maybe not considered by some to be a good one to be found in girls, but I think it is wonderful. Abigail, for all the sunshine that is part of her personality, is also the least sentimental. Through Marnie's family's treatment of Abigail, they crossed some red line with me. When they called her fat and stupid, I could see in her eyes that those words had hurt her, and I wanted to kill them for that. It was because of their treatment of Abigail that I most struggled with my desire for revenge.

Their criticism of her as being stupid was particularly painful, as Abigail was never as academic as her sisters. She took that to mean she wasn't as smart, which I knew wasn't true, so I very carefully managed her last years of high school. I sold the big house and moved into a rental near her school so she could walk there. I insisted she get a job in town. I put her in charge of doing all the grocery shopping for herself. I was pushing her to become more independent. She now became the object of my laser focus.

She watched others in her high school class go off to Ivy League colleges, but she had never tried her best in school. So, I decided to try an experiment, and push her out of her comfort zone. I convinced her to go to school in New York City, where I knew she would become intendent and tough. When we visited, she loved the city, and it was then that I knew then my plan had a chance of succeeding.

The first semester was a little rough on her. She called often asking, "When are you going to come visit?" and "When are we going to dinner?" But by the second semester, she made friends and never came home again. She was as happy as a pig in…mud. She proved to be a straight-A student, took on campus leadership positions, and even got several prestigious internships. Abigail has blossomed and found her niche. She graduated summa cum laude and had a job waiting for her with a Fortune 100 company. She really did make it on her own, although I'm delighted to say that she still calls her dad for advice from time to time. We now live minutes apart in New York City, so dad-daughter dinners happen often.

All my children have grown into the kinds of adults every parent prays theirs will be, and I really had so very little to do with it. Even a guy with my (newly discovered) ego and lack of awareness has to see that help has come from a highly placed Source.

Such favors from the Almighty, I have also come to realize, don't come without repayment. Nobody rides for free. I was asked to show my gratitude—to pay the divine piper—and I was soon given the chance.

I was asked to share my story with a single-parenting group at the synagogue and did so, marveling at how alike the feelings of everyone in the room were. We all faced the same crushing depression, guilt at having allowed such abuse, and soul-destroying fantasies of revenge. We all felt inadequate and ignorant and terrified, and the sharing of those feelings helped not only me but all of us.

My story spread, and I got more speaking engagements and soon was asked to write an article about my experiences for The Good Men Project, The Huffington Post, and Entrepreneur, and from there, I wrote articles and blog posts for many publications and websites. I started a website of my own, msweetwood.com, and began hearing from other parents—single dads and moms and still-married parents who had friends and family members suffering pain like that which my family and I had lived through. I even heard from children who related what I wrote about to their relationships with their dads. My audience grew. Television came calling, and with-it appearances on shows like Fox & Friends and NBC's Today, and on all the major networks.

Someone dubbed me "The Voice of Single Dads," and the name stuck and, judging from the number of emails and calls, became true.

I had been given help, and now the Head Coach was calling me off the bench as a pinch hitter for His other players.

Having stepped out of the dugout at His signal, I have found that my life keeps getting better and better.

CHAPTER 16
A TRICK OR TWO

There was a kid in one of my classes at grade school who learned only from getting in trouble. No matter what the motivation—his parents being proud of him, his parents being angry at him, spending yet another recess in the principal's office, gold stars, red Fs, special tutoring, afternoons in detention—nothing seemed to faze him until his father literally took a belt to him.

To some people, negative attention is better than no attention at all.

While it is true that God had to slap me upside the head plenty in order to get my attention, through trial and error I was able to help myself and my kids learn some lessons without pain being the motivator. It seems as I started to man up, I started to wise up.

Here are a few things I learned and did along the way:

I Realized That Bad Treatment Is Never Acceptable
Whether someone is my acquaintance, friend, or lover, he or she has no right to treat me poorly. If you treat me badly, you do not deserve to be in my life.

I Learned That I Am Worthy of Being Loved
Loving (and marrying) someone doesn't mean that you have to continually earn that person's love and respect. I deserve love and respect just for being the man that I am.

I Stopped Overcompensating as a Parent
When my kids' birth mother left, I felt guilty and pitied them, so I was overprotective, didn't discipline them enough, and didn't provide enough structure. After my second divorce, I was a tougher and more thoughtful parent with the goal of doing what was best to make them successful.

I Realized Material Possessions Don't Provide Happiness
After I realized that my happiness comes from within me, the people who are close to me, and the experiences I choose to have, I was able to look for happiness in the right places.

I Made My Physical Health a Top Priority
Part of taking time for myself is making sure I stay healthy. As I get

older, I work harder to keep myself in good physical condition, because physical strength has always been my foundation for emotional and mental strength.

I Made Time for Myself

I had developed the habit of giving everything I had (and more) to my kids, which took its toll on my mental and physical health. I realized that taking time for myself wasn't selfish but smart. It made me happier, more productive, and more successful—as a businessman and as a parent.

I Found My Spiritual Side

I wasn't very spiritual before my marriages, but faith provided a comforting voice that guided me through those adversities. It gave me the patience and strength to always be there for my children and myself, despite my pain.

I Recognized the Positive Things in My Life

After enduring two failed marriages, raising five children alone and having incredibly strained financial circumstances, it was easy to be negative. I started listing the positive things in my life every day. Eventually the positives started outnumbering the negatives by bigger and bigger margins.

I Recognized That Anger Is a Wasted Emotion

I had accumulated a lot of rage and bitterness from my marriages and divorce proceedings, but very little of it is still with me today. I am in a better place now because I have taken responsibility for my actions and how they contributed to what happened, and because I have accepted that what happened is in the past. All I can do is work on my present and future. While the anger is not completely gone, I work every day to heal and recover. One way I do this is through writing articles, which help others going through similar situations.

I Became Grateful for Everything I Already Have

I am grateful that I have five amazing kids in my life, who continually pay me back with their love and success. I am lucky to say that I have a long list of things I am grateful for, which I add to every week. When I am down, I read it and instantly cheer up.

I Had to Find Kindness Within Me

When it was time for the court-appointed visitations with the kids' mother, I did not impose any ideas upon them, but I listened to them intently when they were done. We talked extensively about their new relationship and our relationship to each other. I did not bad-mouth their mother, which took a tremendous amount of restraint. From the moment she finally exited our lives 20 years ago, Charlotte has made no effort to contact her children. Birthdays, graduations, and even a wedding have slipped by without so much as a phone call or card from her, but she is the one made less by that abandonment. She missed all the stresses and strains of raising her children, but she missed all the incredible joy, too. I am so glad I was there for every second of it all.

I Learned to Forgive

Giving up resentment and becoming willing to forgive even those people who had hurt my children were a huge spiritual task I had to undertake. When I learned to lift that burden from my shoulders, my spirit was able to soar. I made room for love, gratitude, and growth.

I Had to Be Willing to Blaze a Trail

I wanted to run away, but I didn't. I was a pioneer of sorts in the process—I had never seen any man in my neighborhood who had full custody of all his children. Just because I had never heard of another man's doing it didn't mean it could not be done. It could. I just had to stand up for what was right and keep standing, no matter how the winds buffeted me.

I Learned to Be a Man

There are characteristics necessary to be a grown-up instead of a child. Being a male over a certain age isn't enough. I had to absorb some lessons about being a man:

A man is thankful: I am grateful for every day I have had these kids in my life. They are wonderful human beings. I am grateful to be employed, healthy, and able to take care of myself. I am also glad I am no longer so wrapped up in misery that I am blinded to the good things in my life.

A man learns to trust: I trust in something outside of myself. I had never been spiritual before, but when my life as I planned it fell apart, what did I have to lose by trying? The Almighty took that one small crack in the armor that surrounded my broken heart and jimmied His way right inside.

A man is inspirational: I inspire my kids to do their best. I inspire the people I work with. I inspire myself to do my very best every single day— some days better than others, but I never do anything less than aspire to my highest heights.

A man learns to let go of anger: I worked, little by little, at getting over my rage and bitterness. I started taking responsibility for my part in what had happened. I'm not saying I'm 100 percent there, but my writing and my putting my heart and soul into helping other men and women are part of my healing.

A man is desperate: I didn't really know desperation until I had children—in particular when I had to care for them myself. I am desperate for their success—for all five of them to live healthy, happy, and autonomous lives. It is that desperate desire that supplies the willingness to sacrifice, to help get them there.

A man stays physically healthy: I work hard now to keep myself in tip-top physical condition. It's not just about me. It's also about being there for a long time for the ones I love.

A man is humble: I found out I don't control everything. I don't know everything. I'm not the bravest, and I make mistakes. My life is a process, and if I am open to it, I can improve every day.

Life would not have been such a difficult and painful learning experience if I'd had some idea of what was ahead for me.

Here are some things I wish someone had told me about being a man when I was younger:
• It's not just okay but essential to ask for help, and it's smart to walk away from "help" that is unsolicited or seems motivated by the wrong reasons.
• Not everything is straightforward or logical. It's perfectly okay to trust your (fatherly) male instincts.
• Anger is a wasted emotion and drains your energy. Letting go of your anger sets you free and on the path to success.
• Life isn't going to be fair, and things frequently won't work out like they should.
• Overcoming life's biggest problems and challenges is going to provide you with the greatest personal growth.
• Material possessions will not provide happiness. Happiness comes from within you, the people in your life, and the experiences you have.
• Being a father to five children and raising them to successful adults will provide you more happiness and satisfaction than anything else you could have done with your life.

I have spent these past 20 years raising my children as both "Mr. Mom" and "Mr. Dad," while running my business and finding a way to enjoy my photography, play an occasional round of golf, and race my car on the track. I also did it while retaining at least some of my sanity. My list of qualities of what I believe it takes to be a man has evolved, to say the least, and put me on paths I never could have imagined, one of which is writing this book.

My kids are all in their 20s now, and what a long, strange trip it has been. Four have attended top colleges, one is just married, another helps run my former business and, most gratifying to me, all five are successful, happy, and kind human beings despite the odds and the difficulties they faced growing up. We all love each other and stay close to each other and, particularly in this world so full of discord and distance, that means everything to me.

Through all the desperate tears and pain of all those years, I never knew I was truly being not only cared for by an unseen Power, but forged in steel to help others in my same situation stand strong through their times of trial. Yet, despite the ignorance, insensitivity, and intemperance of my past, I am still standing with a loving family, a healed heart, and an open hand to soothe the suffering of other single parents.

You too can come through the fire, scarred but alive, older and finally wiser, ready to face the rest of your life with energy and joy.

In any way I can, I am here for you and happy to help.

EPILOGUE
HIDDEN GIFTS

When I first faced those tear-stained faces of my kids looking up at me, stricken in fear over their mother's violent actions, I felt as though time had stopped. I was frozen in disbelief at what was happening—to me. Not to them. My first thought was about me.

What the hell was I going to do?

I felt like frost had taken over my soul and all I could feel was cold. I saw before me only a bleak future filled with despair, sadness, and isolation. A lifetime alone with all those kids. A lifetime alone. Any notions of joy or health or financial success flew from me like the north wind had blown in.

I couldn't have been more wrong. My children, each in their own way, through their individual triumphs and tragedies, have defined for me the word "blessing."

I have been blessed by being given this path to follow. Without it, and its hardships, I would never have known the indescribable happiness I felt when I kissed a scrape and stopped a tear, helped with a thorny math problem and watched the light of learning appear in my son's eyes, or danced at my daughter's wedding, where her whispered "I love you, Dad. Thank you for everything you've done" swelled my heart near to bursting.

I have felt what could have been an unseen pat on my back when I've shared my story with a parent in pain or listened while parents have shared their own tales with me. I grow each time, as a father, a man, a human being. I am proud that I have finally become a mensch—an upstanding man—not flawless, certainly, but better able to help others because of my flaws.

It has all been, as the villagers sang to Tevye in Fiddler on the Roof, a blessing on my head.

ABOUT THE AUTHOR

Matt Sweetwood is well known as a CEO, a successful entrepreneur, an award winning marketer, a social media influencer and a personal branding expert. Matt was the U.S. CEO of beBee, Inc., a professional social network that helps build successful personal brands. He served as President of Unique Photo®, NJ's premiere Camera Store for 28 years. Nationally known in the photography industry as an innovator, he has helped acquire over fifty U.S. and International Trademarks for both language and design and he founded and ran the Ozzie Award winning publication Photo Insider®. Matt has been credited with the reinvention of the modern camera store, as well as the country's largest in-store education program, the Unique University®. Unique Photo was named 2008 and "2013 Dealer of the Year" by Digital Imaging Reporter magazine. Matt was named the Photo Industry's, "2016 Person of the Year" by the PMDA.

However, by far, his greatest achievement is having raised five successful children to adulthood as a single dad. Matt was awarded full custody of their five children, ages 18 months to 8 years old. In the 25 years since, he has raised his kids, on his own, into happy, successful and kindhearted adults. Matt has gained expertise in a range of issues such as surviving divorce and custody, single-parenting, dating, relationships, getting in shape, but most importantly – how anyone can have a life worth living – a BIG Life – no matter what difficulties he or she faces.

Matt has appeared as a regular contributor on Fox News, NBC Today Show, CBS TV, News 12 NJ, PIX11, and other high-profile programs. He has also spoken publicly for major organizations, and was a member of the prestigious CMO Club, where he won the President's Award in 2014.

Matt's past charitable endeavors include having served as Chairman of the Board of Directors at both The Aish Center, a spiritual/educational non-profit and The Josephine Herrick Project, a nonprofit that uses photography to enhance the lives of the under-served. Matt was honored by The Aish Center with its 2014 Continuity Award.

Proving his contention that single dads can lead exciting, balanced lives, Matt is a die-hard NJ Devils' hockey fan, an advanced auto racer with the BMW Club, and of course, an avid photographer. He is sponsored by Panasonic® in his photographic endeavors as a Lumix Luminary. He received his BA in mathematics from Rutgers University and MA in theoretical mathematics from the University of Pennsylvania and his Ph.D. in computer science from Warnborough College in Ireland.